British Public Opinion

Making Contemporary Britain

General Editor: Anthony Seldon
Consultant Editor: Peter Hennessy

Books in the series

Northern Ireland since 1968
Paul Arthur and Keith Jeffery

The Prime Minister since 1945
James Barber

British General Elections since 1945
David Butler

Britain and the Suez Crisis
David Carlton

The End of the British Empire
John Darwin

British Defence since 1945
Michael Dockrill

Britain and the Falklands war
Lawrence Freedman

Britain and European Integration since 1945
Stephen George

Consensus Politics from Attlee to Thatcher
Dennis Kavanagh and Peter Morris

Britain and the Korean War
Callum Macdonald

Culture in Britain since 1945
Arthur Marwick

Crime and Criminal Justice since 1945
Terence Morris

The British Press and Broadcasting since 1945
Colin Seymour-Ure

British Science and Politics since 1945
Thomas Wilkie

British Public Opinion
Robert M. Worcester

Institute of Contemporary British History
34 Tavistock Square, London WC1H 9EZ

British Public Opinion

A Guide to the History and Methodology of Political Opinion Polling

Robert M. Worcester

Basil Blackwell

First published 1991

Basil Blackwell Ltd
108 Cowley Road, Oxford, OX4 1JF, UK

Basil Blackwell, Inc.
3 Cambridge Center
Cambridge, Massachusetts 02142, USA

British Library Cataloguing in Publication Data

A CIP catalogue record for this book is available from the British Library.

Library of Congress Cataloging in Publication Data

Worcester, Robert M.
  British public opinion : a guide to the history and methodology of public opinion polling/Robert M. Worcester.
      p.   cm. — (Making contemporary Britain)
  Includes bibliographical references and index.
  ISBN 0—631—17058—8 (hardback) ISBN 0—631—17059—6
  1. Public opinion — Great Britain — History — 20th century. 2. Public opinion polls. I. Title. II. Series.
HN400.P8W67 1991
  303.3′8′0941—dc20   90—40347
                                                                          CIP

Typeset in 11 on 13 pt. Ehrhardt
by Setrite Typesetters Ltd, Hong Kong
Printed in Great Britain by Billing & Sons Ltd, Worcester

Contents

vi   *Contents*

General Editor's Preface

The Institute of Contemporary British History's series *Making Contemporary Britain* is aimed directly at students in schools and universities and at others interested in learning more about topics in post-war British history. In the series, authors are less attempting to break new ground than presenting clear and balanced overviews of the state of knowledge on each of the topics.

The ICBH was founded in October 1986 with the objective of promoting the study of British history since 1945 at every level. To that end, it publishes books and a quarterly journal, *Contemporary Record*; it organizes seminars and conferences for school students, undergraduates, researchers and teachers of post-war history; and it runs a number of research programmes and other activities.

A central theme of the ICBH's work is that post-war history is too often neglected in British schools, institutes of higher education and beyond. The ICBH acknowledges the validity of the arguments against the study of recent history, notably the problems of bias, of overly subjective teaching and writing, and the difficulties of perspective. But it believes that the values of studying post-war history outweigh the drawbacks, and that the health and future of a liberal democracy require that its citizens know more about the most recent past of their country than the limited knowledge possessed by British citizens, young and old, today. Indeed, the ICBH believes that the dangers of political

indoctrination are higher where the young are *not* informed of
the recent past.

Opinion polls have become a common and influential feature
of British public life. Yet no one before has brought together in
one volume an account of how political opinion polls emerged
in Britain, the role they have today, and how they should be
used to best effect.

Robert Worcester has the advantage of being a key player in
the story as the head of one of Britain's major polling organizations. Such a position could have its drawbacks in writing a
book of this nature, without showing undue deference to
MORI, or indeed to the Labour party, for whom MORI has
conducted polls for two decades.

The book will appeal to a wide range of readers, from
students of British politics (for public opinion and polls are of
increasing scholarly interest), to journalists who report the polls,
to researchers and businessmen wanting to know more about
why and how to measure public opinion.

Robert Worcester's book should be read in association with
another in the series, by Colin Seymour-Ure, on the media in
Britain since 1945.

Anthony Seldon

Introduction and Acknowledgements

The groundwork for this book originated over a decade ago, and arose out of a perceived need among members of the Council of the World Association for Public Opinion Research (WAPOR) for a comparative study of the history and practice of opinion polling across national boundaries. The first paper that led to this work was presented to a joint conference of the American Association of Public Opinion Research (AAPOR) and WAPOR, its international equivalent, in 1980. Several expansions of that paper followed for various purposes, until it was joined by nine other contributions, also from developed countries, to comprise the chapters of a book published by Macmillan in 1985 entitled *Political Opinion Polling: An International Review*.* That chapter has now been developed, expanded and augmented to become the first part of this current book.

I wish at the outset to once again pay tribute to the splendid post-war Nuffield College Oxford, General Election series. These books cover not only each general election since 1945, but the between-election periods as well. For the most part they are the work of that doyen of psephologists, Dr David Butler, who has made the study of elections and electoral behaviour his life's work. In each of his Nuffield publications

* R. Worcester (ed.), *Political Opinion Polling: An International Review* (Macmillan, 1983; St Martin's Press, 1983).

he has not only documented the findings of the polls and the involvement of the pollsters, but he and his co-authors have provided insight into the perceptions of their use by the politicians in the case of the private polls and the effect of the published polls on both the politicians and the electorate. David's work is always meticulously and thoroughly done, is highly objective and is the epitome of all good connoted by the word 'academic' with none of the bad.

His co-authors, Richard Rose (1959), an expatriate American like myself, the Canadian Anthony King (1964 and 1966), and latterly Dennis Kavanagh (February and October 1974, 1979, 1983 and 1987), have been and continue to be keen students of political opinion polls and willing sources of analysis, advice and critical evaluation of pollsters' work.

David Butler is, of course, the chairman of the editorial board of *Contemporary Record*, the Journal of the Institute of Contemporary History. Wearing this hat he introduced me to Anthony Seldon, General Editor of the Blackwell series, who proposed this book and suggested also that extracts from an earlier draft be published in *Contemporary Record* in 1988–9.*

This book is presented in three sections. Part I, The History of Political Opinion Polling in Great Britain: 1937–1979, briefly chronicles the setting up of the first polling organizations, following on from the establishment of the market research firms which preceded them. Gallup was the first, and celebrated its fiftieth anniversary several years ago. Space will not permit, nor is the reader likely to be interested in the minutia of between-elections polling data in these early days.

Part II, however, Political Opinion Polling in the First Thatcher Decade: 1979–1989, is more detailed. It shows how polling evidence measured the first election of Mrs Margaret Thatcher in 1979, the decline of Tory support in her early years in office and then the remarkable recovery during the Falklands War period. The rise and fall of the Social

---

* R. Worcester 'Political Opinion Polling: Past and Present', *Contemporary Record*, Winter 1988 and 'Political Opinion Polling: Problems and Prospects', *Contemporary Record*, November 1989.

Democratic Party and the SDP/Liberal Alliance, the 1983 General Election, the period in between 1983 and 1987, and then the 1987 election are all treated in some detail.

Part III is mainly methodological and illustrated how the marriage of the art of asking questions with the science of sampling, together with the analysis of the resulting data, leads to accurate and useful measurement of British public opinion. Then follow tips for both the journalist writing up and the reader or viewer appraising opinion poll results in the newspapers and in the broadcast media, for without the distribution of the information polls can provide, they would not serve the public interest.

I would like to express my appreciation to my colleagues who have worked with me over the years on our political surveys. Especial thanks are due to Sarah Green who prepared my index, and to my colleagues in the polling fraternity, both in Britain and abroad, who have provided much professional and intellectual stimulation (especially through WAPOR). Finally, I wish to thank my wife, Margaret, who has shown such patience with my frequent absences, both in person and in mind, while I have been preoccupied with my work.

Robert M. Worcester
London, October 1990

Part I
The History of Political Opinion Polling in Great Britain: 1937–1979

1 The Early Days: Founding Fathers

British Gallup, originally known as BIPO (British Institute of Public Opinion), was the first organization of its kind in Britain, being founded in 1937, just two years after its American fore-father. Its poll findings were published in the *News Chronicle* until that paper's demise in 1960 and have since then been published regularly in the *Daily Telegraph*. Gallup polls were conducted monthly until the mid 1950s, and at least weekly, although only published once a month, since then. Gallup's findings have been published more extensively in its monthly *Gallup Political Index*, which has been running for more than 20 years.

Its poll findings on all sorts of topics for the years 1937–75 are published in two fat, useful and frequently amusing books.[1] In the early days most questions were of the 'Yes/No' variety, at first covering such topics as divorce, mercy killings, compulsory military training and recognition of Franco's junta in Spain. Among the first few questions asked were these, which do, indeed, make fascinating reading:

If you had to choose between Fascism and Communism, which would you choose?

	%
Fascism	49
Communism	51

(46% expressed no opinion)

Source: Gallup, 1937

Should Great Britain remain a member of the League of Nations?

	%
Yes	84
No	16

(14% expressed no opinion)

Source: Gallup, 1937

and

Have you ever travelled to America?

	%
Yes	8
No	92

Source: Gallup, 1937

Interestingly, MORI asked a similar question in 1979 for *Now!* magazine[2] and found a similar 8% of the British public at that time saying they had ever visited the United States.

Some questions asked in 1938 have considerable relevance today: they include questions on the reunification of Ireland, devolution in Scotland and participation in football pools. Others began the series of political questions that continue today, first, in October 1938, on the public's satisfaction with Mr Neville Chamberlain as Prime Minister (57% satisfied, 43% dissatisfied, 10% no opinion). Mrs Thatcher, who in March 1990 had just 20% satisfied with her performance, would be delighted with those figures now.

The first voting intention question was introduced in February 1939, when 64% answered that they would vote for the government 'if there were a general election tomorrow' and 36% for the opposition − 16% no opinion. In March of that year a question was posed asking 'If Mr Chamberlain retires, whom would you like to be Prime Minister?' Mr Anthony Eden was all odds the popular choice with 38%, Lord Halifax and Winston

Churchill, the real choice when the crunch did come, got 7% each. But a majority, 56%, did favour Churchill being invited to join the Cabinet.

Gallup's first associate in Britain was the late Dr Henry Durant, who reminisced some years ago how he began polling in the first place.

> I had taken my degree at LSE. As usual in the early 30s no job: I lectured, was registered for a PhD, was writing, earning money any way I could. Not Gallup himself, but an associate of his, Harry Field, came from the USA in 1936 looking for somebody to start up part time Gallup work from home. He went to LSE Appointments Bureau, was given half-a-dozen names and he chose mine; just like that. For a lordly £150 per year I did postal surveys, till the *News Chronicle* became interested. They said, 'We want you to forecast the by-election to show that the system works.' West Fulham: Edith Summerskill was Labour candidate. It was a Conservative seat and she upset the Conservative, as I had forecast, and by a miracle I got it on the nose within 1%; beginner's luck.[3]

It was certainly to some degree luck, and also to some degree sampling skill, as was proved some years later, following the war. During the war, Dr Durant and his colleagues were largely focused on government work, testing morale and public acceptance of various schemes, but they continued to publish their poll findings regularly in the sparse pages of the *News Chronicle* during those paper-rationed times.

Durant's heart was, however, in political polling. Durant: 'When the General Election came, in May '45, Gallup showed that Attlee was going to win with the Labour Party. Nobody believed us, including all the News Chronicle people.'

Neither were they believed by Conservative Central Office. According to the Prime Minister, Winston Churchill, the view of Central Office was that the Tories should be returned with a substantial majority. According to Churchill's own account:

> I had not burdened myself unduly with the subject [of the election] while occupied with the grave business of the [Potsdam] conference. On the whole I accepted the view of the party managers and went to bed in the belief that the British people would wish me to continue my work. My hope was that it would

be possible to reconstitute the National Coalition Government in the proportions of the new House of Commons. Thus slumber. However, just before dawn I woke suddenly with a sharp stab of almost physical pain. A hitherto subconscious conviction that we were beaten broke forth and dominated by mind ... I was discontented at the prospect, and turned over and went to sleep again.[4]

We have the recollection of Lord Moran,[5] Churchill's doctor, who reports that in a conversation with the then former Prime Minister in the year after the great man's defeat, he tried to argue that Churchill's defeat was only the swing of the pendulum, but finding Churchill's mind elsewhere, told him of the Gallup polls carried out at intervals throughout the war by the *News Chronicle* and when he did, got Churchill's attention: 'Tell me about them,' Churchill commanded. Moran says he told Churchill that 'two questions were put to the readers (sic). To the first, "Who do you think should be responsible for the conduct of the war" there was only one answer: "Winston Churchill." The second brought out their hostility to the Tories. Churchill interrupted at this point, "I don't understand."' Moran reported that he then said that all the time the percentage of voters who wanted a Tory government after the war was steadily falling. Churchill had been listening intently. 'And then, as he mused, the light went out of his face.'

Gallup in the United States began as a means of journalism, as did its British offspring in Britain. As Dr Durant explained:

'People constantly asked us to put questions on our regular surveys and at the beginning I was stupid enough to regard these as a nuisance: then I suddenly realised that this was a beautiful way of making money. It grew and soon had its own omnibus survey: today it's one of the things that researchers live off.'[6]

BIPO's performance at the 1945 General Election was certainly creditable. It was, of course, the only player on the field. There were no precedents in this country, although the American Institute of Public Opinion, led by Dr Gallup, had performed well at both the 1936 and 1940 American Presidential elections. The Gallup people here, led by Dr Durant, suggested a lead of 6% for Labour while the outcome was in fact 9.5%, possibly

TALKING POINT

Doing Fine

ON the front page today is printed another interim forecast by the Gallup Poll of how people are proposing to vote. This is based on a sample taken in a large number of constituencies between June 24 and June 27.

This sample does not pretend to foretell the result of the election. A Gallup forecast of the final result would only be possible if a poll were taken in each of these constituencies.

All the same the results are illuminating. They are, in one sense, encouraging from Labour's point of view. They show that a higher proportion of the total electorate is proposing to vote Labour than was the case when the last Gallup Poll was published a fortnight ago. But also on a closer analysis, they are even more encouraging from the point of view of the Liberal Party.

Compared with a Gallup Poll taken a fortnight earlier, the number of voters who declare their intention of voting Liberal has dropped

SECOND GALLUP ELECTION POLL

Labour's 6-point lead

IN its second election survey, completed on Wednesday of last week, the Gallup Poll tested the voting intentions of the civilian electorate.

A representative sample of men and women voters covering 195 constituencies were asked the following question:

"For which candidate do you intend to vote in the General Election?"

47.0 said Labour.

the Liberal programme would indicate a 20 per cent. preference throughout the constituencies as a whole.

The inference is unmistakable. In face of the handicap of our irrational electoral system, and of the discouragements of the inter-war years, there is a notable revival of enthusiasm for the Liberal cause. The Party's programme, as expounded during the present contest, is daily winning new adherents.

Tomorrow, at the Polls, every Liberal must cast his vote, so as to prove beyond the contradiction of opponents that Liberalism is coming into its own again.

41.0 said Conservative (or Nat. or Lib. Nat.)
10.5 said Liberal
0.5 said Communist.
0.5 said Common Wealth
0.5 said Others.

These results are naturally affected by the voting possibilities open to the individual voter. To take the most obvious example, while in most constituencies voters have an opportunity to vote for a Conservative or for a Labour candidate, in less than one half of the constituencies will Liberal voters have the chance of voting for a Liberal candidate.

Thus, though the figure of 10.5 per cent. given above represents the probable proportion of Liberal votes in the total poll throughout the country, the proportion of Liberal votes in constituencies where there are Liberal candidates will be considerably higher.

The indications of this survey are that the Liberal vote, averaged out over all the constituencies where there are Liberal candidates, is likely to be slightly over 20 per cent.

The same factor, of course, also operates in the cases of the smaller parties.

    ★

It must be emphasised that it is impossible to base upon these

Yet, paradoxical as it may seem, the results actually prove that the Liberal cause has been making marked headway.

The explanation is that when the last Gallup Poll was taken the electors stated their electoral preferences without knowing which parties would run candidates in their constituencies. But the present Poll was taken *after Nomination Day*, when very many people who would vote Liberal if they could have no Liberal candidate in their constituency to vote for.

It is only possible to vote Liberal in, roughly, one out of every two constituencies; so that a 10.5 per cent. preference for

results any forecast as to the probable distribution of **seats** among the various parties in the new House of Commons which will be returned by the election.

For example, in the 1935 election Labour polled 38 per cent. of the total **votes** cast, but received only 25 per cent. of the **seats** in the House. In that election it took 59,000 Labour votes to return a Labour candidate, while it took only 29,000 "National" votes to return a Government candidate.

If conditions similar to 1935 should operate in the coming election, it might mean that Labour's 47 per cent. of **votes** forecast for them would give them only about 200 **seats**—i.e., a minority.

On the other hand, in the 1929 election, Labour's 37 per cent. of the total **votes** cast gave them 47 per cent. of the **seats** in the House. Under conditions parallel to 1929, Labour's 47 per cent. of **votes** forecast for the present election may give them as many as 370 **seats**—i.e., a majority.

These examples show how unpredictable is the result of a British election under the present voting system.

The above results are based on interviews with **civilian** voters only in 195 constituencies dis-

tributed throughout England, Scotland and Wales. No Northern Ireland constituencies were included. University and business votes were not taken into account. Each person interviewed, therefore, is considered as voting once only.

Service men or women were **not** questioned. There are indications, however, that the Service vote will make to the final result are unlikely to be very great.

Men and women voters in the various age and income groups were sampled in their appropriate numbers.

There is substantial evidence to show that more than one million men and women have been inadvertently omitted from the electoral register for the present election. They will therefore be unable to vote. There is no means of assessing the possible effect of these omissions, since until such persons go to the Poll most of them will not, in fact, discover that they have no vote.

Persons indicating to interviewers that they did not intend to vote in the present election amounted to 11 per cent. of the men and 17 per cent. of the women. These have been excluded in arriving at the above results.

East End gave Premier stormy passage, and the boos he asked for

Table 1.1   General Election, 1945

Poll Newspaper Fieldwork	Gallup *News Chronicle* 24–27 Jun	Actual result 5 Jul
	%	%
Con	41.0	39.3
Lab	47.0	48.8
Lib	10.5	9.2
Other	1.5	2.7
Lab lead	+6.0	+9.5
Error on lead	−3.5	
Average error on share (+/−)	1.5	
Maximum error	1.8	

widened by the large postal vote from servicemen abroad. Table 1.1, however, shows that the final Gallup poll share of each party, taken in 195 constituencies, was nicely within the quite acceptable range of plus or minus 2%.

The General Election of 1950

The polls at the British General Election of 1950 were close, even if two out of three called the wrong winner, and seemed to overcome the scepticism towards the polls resulting from the Dewey–Truman fiasco in the United States in 1948. Three national morning newspapers took the mood of the electorate in the period preceding election day. At that election to poll latest led to closest — something that tended to be overlooked two decades later.

A Gallup survey the preceding October showed an 11% Conservative lead; then on 20 January, following dissolution, a sharp narrowing to 2.5%. The next poll was published on the 30th, and showed Labour moving into a 1.5% lead; Labour's share increased by 17 February, when a 2.5% Labour lead was reported, taken about ten days before polling day.

The first *Daily Express* poll of public opinion was published on 23 January, with a 6% Conservative lead, wider by 3.5% than Gallup was showing at about the same time. A 5% Conservative lead was published on the 30th, widening the gap between themselves and Gallup by 6.5% and forecasting, as it turned out, which poll would be closest on election day (see Table 1.2 on page 11).

The first poll by the *Daily Mail* also appeared, presaging the establishment a few years later of National Opinion Polls (NOP) by the then circulation manager of the *Mail*, Mick Shields.

The General Election of 1951

The political parties first put their toe in the water of polling in the run-up to the 1950 election. All the parties employed pollsters, and the Liberals were first to leak favourable findings, referring to the '38% of the electorate who would vote Liberal if they thought they really could have a Liberal Government'.[7] The Conservatives had also leaked Gallup findings, referring to the '38% of trade union members who intended to vote Conservative at the next election'. For the first time, polling analysis, public and private, became one of the recognized adjuncts of political planning.

During the 1950s, politicians began to take political polls seriously. This was evidenced by the statement by Morgan Phillips, the General Secretary of the Labour party, who warned against 'a new technique of propaganda ... the publication of polls'.[8]

Nearly a quarter of a century later the Labour party was still hounding the pollsters (although graciously making a nod in MORI's direction), saying in its 1974 Report:

Throughout the campaign the opinion polls indicated a heavy

swing against Labour and, of course, proved once again to be totally incorrect. It would also seem that the opinion polls published in the press had a considerable effect in increasing the Liberal vote ... Our own private (MORI) polls were accurate to a high degree and the findings of these polls, which were presented to the Campaign Committee each morning, were of great value.[9]

Three other polls appeared during the 1950s. The *Daily Express*, schizophrenic then as now about polls, conducted its own, yet lumbered it in 1959 with an 'endorsement' that 'The *Daily Express* has no confidence in its own poll, although it is conducted with complete integrity and all possible efficiency'.[10]

The narrow seven-seat lead by the Labour party ensured an early return to the electorate, and it was to come less than two years later. For most of 1950 the mood of the electorate remained stable. Labour had a 3% lead at the election and held their lead throughout the year. As the new year, 1951, turned so did the fortunes of the parties in the polls: in the Gallup poll in February 1951 the Tories jumped first into a 13% lead, holding their lead between 7% and 10% until September.

The *Daily Mail* dropped out of the polling business for the moment, but Research Services Ltd, under the redoubtable Dr Mark Abrams, entered the fray. The outcome for RSL and their client, the *Daily Graphic*, was not too happy either for themselves or for the Conservatives whom they had tipped to win.

To some degree, according to David Butler,[11] their failure was foreseeable. Their estimate for the Liberal and other candidates obviously made inadequate allowance for the small number of seats being fought and on 22 October the regional 'predictions' they offered were, according to Butler, patently absurd. Yet they wrote in the accompanying copy to their first published poll that 'We may be a little out. It will be surprising if we are not, but it will be by no more than a couple of points.' A brave statement with fieldwork conducted a fortnight before polling day.

The *Daily Express* poll, it was plain, had too many 'don't knows' and was not doing enough to sift the preferences of

Table 1.2 General Election, 1950

Poll Newspaper Fieldwork	Own Daily Mail 5–11 Feb	Own Daily Express 17–21 Feb	Gallup News Chronicle 17–20 Feb	Actual result 23 Feb
	%	%	%	%
Con	45.5	45.0	43.5	43.0
Lab	42.5	44.0	45.0	46.8
Lib (+ others)	(12.0)	10.0	10.5	9.3
Others	n/a	1.0	1.0	0.9
Lab lead	−3.0	−1.0	+1.5	+3.8
Error on lead	−6.8	−4.8	−2.3	(4.6)
Average error on share (+/−)	2.9	1.4	0.9	(1.7)
Maximum error	4.3	2.8	1.8	(3.0)

these undecided voters to make an accurate forecast, the error made nearly 30 years later by RSL for the *Observer* when, in the 1979 General Election, acting on the advice of one of Butler's later co-authors, Dr Anthony King, RSL asked only the primary voting intention question without a 'leaner' follow-up. All made the error of quitting too soon, Gallup's last interviews being done three days before polling day.

It was notable that the opinion polls received far more attention by the media and by the politicians than ever before. They depressed Labour at the beginning of the election campaign and perhaps made the Conservatives overconfident. One politician unconvinced clearly by either the large Tory lead and the results of by-elections during 1951 was Prime Minister Clement Attlee, who had sufficient resolution to call the election in the face of a 10% Conservative lead in the Gallup poll and 13% in the *Daily Express* and a set of by-election results that had a median swing of 5.7% from the 1950 election which if it had been replicated that October would have given the Tories an 8% majority of votes or about 180 seats. He went to the country, announcing the election on 19 September, and was rewarded for his bravado in the face of the electoral evidence by losing out to Mr Winston Churchill's Conservative party in seats in the House in spite of out-polling the Tories by some 231,000 votes in the country. (We should note in passing another innovation in election tactics introduced in the 1951 election – the use of party election broadcasts, one allocated to each party.)

The short-lived *Daily Graphic* employed Research Services to run detailed poll coverage giving space to tables of not only top-line totals but age, sex, regional subgroups and to the most important issues influencing the response to their voting decision question. Their text introducing the series of daily polls expressed their pride in their innovation: 'The figures – the very exciting figures you will agree – published on this page are not guesses. They are based upon the most careful, accurate and scientific investigation, carried out on behalf of the *Daily Graphic* by Research Services, Ltd.' They published a series of polls every day from 19 October until 24 October.

Table 1.3   General Election, 1951

Poll	RSL	Own	Gallup[a]	
Newspaper	*Daily Graphic*	*Daily Express*	*News Chronicle*	Actual result
Fieldwork	n/a	19−23 Oct	22 Oct	25 Oct
	%	%	%	%
Cons	50.0	50.0	49.5	48.0
Lab	43.0	46.0	47.0	48.8
Lib (+ others)	(7.0)	3.5	3.5	2.5
Others		0.5	0.5	0.7
Lab lead	−7.0	−4.0	−2.5	+0.8
Error on lead	−7.8	−4.8	−3.3	(5.3)
Average error on share (+/−)	3.9	1.5	1.1	(2.2)
Maximum Error	5.8	2.8	1.8	(3.5)

[a] Gallup figures as published add to 100.5%.

The General Elections of 1955 and 1959

The unhappy period in office for an old and ill Winston Churchill finally gave way to an equally unhappy period in office for Sir Anthony Eden, which bracketed the 1955 General Election. With Churchill's resignation on 5 April, it was only ten days until the new Prime Minister called the election for 26 May.

From the outset there was the expectation of a Conservative victory. The Gallup poll published in the *News Chronicle* on 21 April showed the government with a 4% lead over Labour. Perhaps more telling were figures published the following day, which showed that 52% of the public thought that the Conservatives would win and only 22% thought Labour would, and that 83% of Tory intenders expected their party to win while less than half, 49%, of Labour supporters thought their party would win. Within a week however, in a poll published on 28 April, Gallup showed the parties level-pegging. By 5 May however, there was a swing back to the Conservatives. From then, the Tory lead stabilized at around a 3–4% Tory lead for the last fortnight of the campaign.

Butler[12] reports that there is no doubt that the findings of the polls were more influential than in previous campaigns in shaping the thinking of the politicians and, perhaps, the electorate. On 21 May Labour's Herbert Morrison complained that Gallup polls made the public feel that the election was a sort of game, and reduced the extent to which people worked in the campaign, but he did not challenge their findings.

The influence of television grew as the penetration of sets throughout the country deepened, but neither on television, which pretended the election did not exist, nor in the press, was the election the dominant theme that it has become in recent years. During the three weeks between the dissolution of Parliament and polling day election news had priority in the *Manchester Guardian* on only four occasions, in the *Daily Telegraph* on only three, in *The Times* just twice, and in the *News Chronicle* three times, twice when trumpeting the results of its Gallup polls. The *Daily Express* led with election news five times, twice with its poll results, and the popular papers discovered the election as a lead story only in the last three days of the campaign.

The *Daily Express* conducted a regular, if tendentious, poll among its readers to determine their reactions to each political television broadcast, and Harold Macmillan is recorded as noting with pleasure that 'a Gallup poll gave Macmillan 41 marks out of 100 as a performer; Attlee got only 28'.[13] The *Daily Express* published neither fieldwork dates nor sample sizes in its reports. Nor, surprisingly, did the *News Chronicle* publish fieldwork dates, methodology or sample size of their Gallup polls. Nevertheless, the pollsters had cause to be pleased with their performance (see Table 1.4).

David Butler, in an article published in 1955,[14] described election behaviour studies as of long duration, if shallow understanding. Before 1872, party agents had known who had voted

Table 1.4   General Election, 1955

Poll Newspaper Fieldwork	Own *Daily* *Express* n/a	Gallup *News* *Chronicle* 21−24 May*a	Actual result 26 May
	%	%	%
Con	50.2	51.0	49.7
Lab	47.2	47.5	46.4
Lib	2.2	1.5	2.7
Others	0.4	0.0	1.2
Lab lead	−3.0	−3.5	−3.3
Error on lead	0.3	−0.2	(0.25)
Average error on share (+/−)	0.65	1.2	(0.9)
Maximum error	0.8	1.3	(1.1)

*a Fieldwork dates supplied by Robert Wybrow of Gallup in a letter to the author dated 20 March 1990.

and how, and 'Ever since the Reform Bill [1832], Tadpoles and Tapers have been speculating busily on what national "cries" would go down best with the electorate, and what detailed techniques in constituency organization would yield the biggest vote.' In 1955, in his pessimistic article in the *British Journal of Sociology*, Butler said:

> The academic study of elections is still young ... Before the Second World War no-one in the universities had devoted detailed attention to the conduct of contemporary elections or to their results ... The real stimulus to research in voting behaviour was, of course, the advent of the sample survey ... Doubts have grown up about whether either the detailed investigation of the conduct of the campaign, or the elaborate sample survey, offer much prospect of yielding major new discoveries. Briefly, it can be argued that the conduct of the campaign has remarkably little influence on the results of the election, while the practical limits of sample surveys made it unlikely that they

have enormous further contributions to make to exposing either the facts of voting behaviour or the motives behind it.[15]

In 1957 R. M. P. Shields, the late Managing Director of Associated Newspapers (AN), set up National Opinion Polls (NOP) as an AN subsidiary under his own active chairmanship until his death in 1988. It was directed first by Peter Hyatt, a statistician, and on his departure jointly by Frank Teer and John Barter between 1966 and 1972 and subsequently by John Barter alone until 1989 when it was sold by Associated Newspapers to MAI who brought in their own chief executive. NOP originally regularly and then occasionally published its polls in Associated Newspapers' *Daily Mail, Mail on Sunday* and *London Evening Standard* until its sale, and at the beginning of 1990 began a regular polling series with the *Independent*. It also publishes a bi-monthly *Review* of its poll findings. One footnote to history is that like Durant, Shields, Teer and Barter all were graduates of the London School of Economics.

NOP's first General Election poll was in 1959, supplementing its resources with interviewers and tabulating machines made available by the Gallup poll, much to the consternation of the *Observer*, which headlined its Sunday paper 'Four Polls from one Source'.[16]

The *Daily Mail* story on 8 October reported the NOP findings without reallocating the 'don't knows', and published no fieldwork dates, sample sizes or methodological information nor was a follow-up 'squeeze' question reported, if indeed one was asked.

The *Daily Express* published two polls in the last few days of the campaign, the first on 6 October, reporting fieldwork dates of 1–4 October; they then published a poll two days later without noting the (later?) fieldwork dates. Neither reallocated 'don't knows' thus making it impossible for the ordinary reader to comprehend the change, as the first of the pair had 6% still undecided, the final poll reporting 12%, appearing to drop both the Tory and Labour party share of vote by 3% each. The *Express* said 'it publishes this last poll result with complete confidence in the good faith of the poll organisation [sic] and with no [sic] great confidence in the value of this forecast'.

Table 1.5 General Election, 1959

Poll Newspaper Fieldwork	NOP Daily Mail 2–5 Oct[b]	F. Stat[a] Daily Telegraph 1–4 Oct	Own Daily Express n/a	Gallup News Chronicle 3–6 Oct	Actual result 8 Oct
	%	%	%	%	%
Con	48.0	48.6	49.1	48.5	48.8
Lab	44.1	45.7	45.4	46.5	44.6
Lib (+ others)	(7.9)	5.1	5.0	4.5	6.1
Others		0.6	0.5	0.5	0.6
Lab lead	−3.9	−2.9	−3.7	−2.0	−4.2
Error on lead	+0.3	+1.3	+0.5	−2.2	(1.1)
Average error on share (+/−)	0.8	0.6	0.6	1.0	(0.8)
Maximum error	0.8	1.0	1.1	1.9	(1.3)

[a] Forecasting Statistics, a sister company to Gallup. Details supplied by Robert Wybrow of Gallup in a letter to the author dated 20 March 1990.

[b] Estimated by NOP, letter to the author, 22 May 1990.

According to Butler and Rose,[17] the *Observer*'s caveat did not seem to diminish the interest with which the polls were followed.

> Election day was October 8; from September 21 onwards polling results in sponsoring papers (no cross-reporting) began to encourage the Labour Party and to shake up the Tories. What had been a 6.8% Tory lead slid down to around 2%, and three days before polling Gallup reported a neck-and-neck race in the *News Chronicle*. In earlier elections the polls had tended to under-estimate Labour's strength. Yet the popular belief that the Conservatives would win did not fluctuate greatly, with a steady three-to-one majority expecting this at every stage in the campaign. Business (City) opinion was more attuned then as now [see pp. 100−1 and 202−3] to the polls' reports. Stock prices fell on mornings when opinion polls showed a decline in the Tory lead.

Butler and Rose suggest that, while before 1959 polls had an appreciable effect on the morale and expectations of politicians, they had little impact on the electorate. In 1959, however, there were signs of wider impact. Curiously, it was the detractors from the polls rather than their sponsors who ascribed great influence to them: 'Labour supporters were given heart by the appearance of the polls as they reported Labour gains. During this election there were "one or two" voices raised in favour of the suppression or regulation of poll forecasts.' But, Butler and Rose concluded: 'It does not appear that people jump on the winning band-wagon − or even that they side with the underdog ... it is also true that the turnout may be increased by signs that the rivals are neck-and-neck ... the effect of the polls, like that of television, seems to be to stir up interest, and hence participation in the election.' They also concluded that:

> What is also needed is a higher degree of education about the limitations and possibilities of the polls and perhaps more information and humility from some of their sponsors. The first thing that has to be learnt is that their main value does not lie primarily in election prediction. The sampling of opinion can yield a vast amount of information of the greatest political and social importance − and such information, to be valuable, need not be nearly as precise as election forecasts must be. Through

opinion polling, political parties and students of politics can find out in detail the views of different sections of the public, instead of simply guessing at them, or making inferences. Voting is only the end product of a series of influences. Polls will also be most valuable in discovering, not how people are going to vote, but why they vote as they do. Polls can reveal how well informed the public is about any issue and whether it has strong views; they can also reveal what people do and what media of communication they are exposed to. There has never been anything comparable to sample polls as a tool for advancing understanding of mass political behaviour.[18]

In these early days of television, the BBC, then a monopoly, did not report election campaigns at all as a matter of policy. By 1959, the Corporation had reversed this stance. Butler himself, with Donald Stokes,[19] was to publish the key work on electoral behaviour in 1969, some fourteen years after his gloomy prediction for the future of sample surveys in 1955, as well as going on to co-author (to date) another seven volumes in the Nuffield series.

Another valuable commentary on polls and politics — of an international flavour — was offered by Durant[20] in the *British Journal of Sociology*, showing how polls (starting with the National Peace Ballot of 1935 with over 11.5 million respondents) were taken in Britain to measure public attitudes to Britain's conduct of foreign affairs.

Sample overkill was not only a pre-war phenomenon. In 1957 the National Association of Local Government Officials surveyed more than 300,000 households, using 15,000 local council employees, on what people knew and thought of local government,[21] and in 1958−9 Mr Colin Hurry spent some £450,000, partly financed by the then independent steel companies, to 'interview' some 1,948,314 electors in 129 marginal constituencies about their views on nationalization. An editorial in *Political Opinion Quarterly* in 1959 summed up the criticisms made of this method of attempting to influence public opinion:

The wording as well as the sense of certain questions was ... heavily loaded ... The questions were worded in such a way that they would almost certainly evoke prejudices against

nationalisation in many of the persons asked to answer them . . .
The scheme aimed at influencing voters in every area where
they might exert the maximum effect at the coming General
Election.[22]

In 1951, as noted above, Research Services Limited (RSL)
published its first polls during the time its Chairman, Dr Mark
Abrams, was a visiting lecturer at the University of Chicago.
When he returned, he took over responsibility for public opinion
polling at RSL and it was he who during the 1950s and 1960s
conducted private polls for the Labour party.[23] When Dr Abrams
left RSL to become a civil servant, before the 1970 General
Election, there was a hiatus in RSL's political polling work
until its re-entry into the field in 1979 (see p. 66).

Hugh Gaitskell became Leader of the Labour party in
December 1955, following the resignation of former Prime
Minister Clem Attlee, who resigned on the morning of
Wednesday 7 December without trying to warn Herbert
Morrison or Nye Bevan, both of whom were hoping to succeed
him.[24] Supporters of each were more concerned with keeping
the other out than with electing their man, and Gaitskell was
the compromise choice.

Gaitskell had been a lecturer in Economics at University
College, London, and when approached after his election by
John, now Lord, Harris (who became his personal assistant
and press aide in the 1959 election) and by Transport House
researcher, later MP, David Ginsburg to undertake further
research into Labour party policies, he quickly acceded, fighting
an uphill battle for funding with both Bevan and Morrison,
each of whom were suspicious of polling and hostile to spending
any of the party's resources on research.[25]

Both Harris and Ginsburg were very active in organizing
and using polling data within Transport House (the Labour
party HQ) on behalf of both Gaitskell and later Harold
Wilson. Abrams's first survey was for Gaitskell personally, and
aroused considerable interest in the Labour Leader. Ginsburg
and Abrams proposed a second, to focus on the perceived
strengths and weaknesses of Gaitskell personally. Gaitskell
turned it down sharply, lecturing the pair of advisers that he

thought it an inappropriate subject for research, and that he did not wish them to consider surveying him as opposed to the party. After a 1957 survey on the views of young people, Abrams appeared in a party political broadcast which dealt with the subject.

Abrams then was also conducting surveys for 'Socialist Commentary'; the first one, written with Richard Rose, resulted in a 'Penguin Special' publication in 1960.[26] It had considerable impact on Labour politics of the day, reportedly especially on the thinking of Anthony Crosland, who always took a keen interest in polling results.

Notes

1 G. Gallup (ed.), *The Gallup International Public Opinion Polls, Great Britain*, 1937–1975 (Random House, 1976).

2 MORI survey, 'Why the British are Still a World Apart', *Now!*, 1 February 1980, pp. 20–5.

3 B. Chappell, 'Founding Fathers: Henry Durant', Market Research Society Newsletter, nos 157–8, April–May 1979.

4 Winston Churchill, *The Second World War, vol. VI, Triumph and Tragedy* (Cassel, 1954).

5 Lord Moran, *Winston Churchill: The Struggle for Survival 1940–1965* (Constable, 1966).

6 Chappell, 'Founding Fathers'.

7 H. G. Nicholas, *The British General Election of 1950* (Macmillan, 1951).

8 Mark Abrams, *Social Surveys and Social Action* (Heinemann, 1951).

9 Report of the National Executive Committee of the Labour Party, 1974, p. 3.

10 Frank Teer and James Spence, *Political Opinion Polls* (Hutchinson University Library, 1973).

11 David Butler, *The British General Election of 1951* (Macmillan, 1952).

12 David Butler, *The British General Election of 1955* (Macmillan, 1955).

13 A. Horne, *Macmillan: 1894–1956* (Macmillan, 1988).

14 David Butler, 'Voting Behaviour and its Study in Britain', *British Journal of Sociology*, 6, 1955, pp. 93–103.
15 Ibid.
16 David Butler and Richard Rose, *The British General Election of 1959* (Macmillan, 1960).
17 Ibid.
18 Ibid.
19 David Butler and Donald Stokes, *Political Change in Britain*, 2nd edn (Macmillan, 1969).
20 Henry Durant, 'Public Opinion, Polls and Foreign Policy', *British Journal of Sociology*, 13, 1962, pp. 331–49.
21 'NALGO survey by more than 15,000 Local Council Employees of over 15,000 homes. What they know and think of Local Government', *The Times*, 2 April, 1957, p 12.
22 W. Robson, 'The Survey on Nationalisation', Political Quarterly, Vol. 30, No 2, April-June 1959, p. 111.
23 Teer and Spence, *Political Opinion Polls*.
24 Philip Williams, *Hugh Gaitskell* (Jonathan Cape, 1979).
25 Mark Abrams, Letter to the author, 15 March 1990.
26 Mark Abrams and Richard Rose, *Must Labour Lose?* (Penguin, 1960).

2 The Middle Years: Coming of Age

During the 1960s, polls in Britain began to come of age. Several new organizations entered the field, regular private polls were commissioned by the political parties, 'sensible' polling started being used by pressure groups, and newspapers (and television) began to take the polls much more seriously.

Opinion Research Centre (ORC) was established by T. F. Thompson and Humphrey Taylor in 1965, with the Conservative party as its first major client. Their main newspaper clients were the *Evening Standard*, the *Scotsman*, *The Times* and the *Sunday Times*. Thompson had worked at Conservative Central Office and Taylor had been head of the political polling section at NOP, which was then doing the private polling for the Conservative party. Thompson and Taylor were both critical of the attempts made by the Conservative party in the field of survey research in 1964.

The Tories had first employed survey research in 1958 in the Rochdale by-election, which may have been then, as now, in possible violation of the Representation of the People Act as an election expense, and in excess of the allowable expenditure. Their advertising agency, CPV (Coleman, Prentiss and Varley), employed research techniques in the 1959 elections, but these were largely ignored by Conservative party leaders (CPV were reported to have spent less than £5,000 on polls). In the early 1960s, the Tories had some work done for them by NOP

(Taylor was then an NOP employee), and in 1963 conducted a 10,000-case study, the major emphasis of which was to identify Conservative defectors, measure attitudes towards the two major parties, and the leaders. Reports show that presentation of these findings confused rather than clarified the situation at Tory Central Office. Of course, this was in large part due to the leadership struggle which occupied Tory attentions for the best part of 1963. From May 1963 to October 1964 the Conservatives reportedly spent about £10,000 on survey research.[1]

Mark Abrams, Chairman of RSL, began work for the Labour party when Hugh Gaitskell was Leader, as noted in Chapter 1, and continued work for Labour under Harold Wilson until the end of the decade. Dr Abrams was widely recognized as a committed social democrat, and the acceptance of his work in Labour party circles suffered as a result. His first work to appear was on party policy (a forbidden area of inquiry later in the 1970s when Tony Benn was involved in the questionnaire design), and, to a lesser extent, on the party's image. Only 400 electors were interviewed, and the results regarded as preliminary. A study (on education) was conducted the following year, however, with Gaitskell's support. Attitudes to issues was what Gaitskell was after, and Abrams's studies were concerned with immigration, comprehensive schools and the values held by new voters. When Enoch Powell was making his speeches about the consequences of immigration, Abrams showed respondents seven of Powell's statements, without attribution, and asked for the respondents' views, and then their party support. Unsurprisingly, a majority of Labour supporters were in agreement with the Powell viewpoint. The reaction of the then General Secretary of the Labour party, Len Williams, was typical: 'Damned waste of money; I could have told you that without a survey.'

Further research was proposed in 1957, but Nye Bevan, as Deputy Leader and party Treasurer, opposed the plan (as Treasurer Norman Atkinson did in 1979), and then Gaitskell dropped the idea. Abrams reflected on Labour's failure to employ survey research effectively in an article in 1964:

Perhaps the most important reason why the Labour party failed, in the 1950s, to engage in public opinion surveys was that the exercise could have led nowhere. The party simply had no machinery that could have taken survey findings and used them to help shape effective political propaganda. It made sense for the Conservatives to commission research, because under the unchallenged and unchallengeable authority of the Party's informal liaison committee there was built a communications machine that digested survey findings. Nothing comparable existed in the Labour Party.[2]

In the 1960s, Nye Bevan's death removed an intractable opponent of opinion polls; Morgan Phillips retired in 1961, and a new General Secretary – and publicity officer – were appointed at Labour party headquarters. These changes led to Mark Abrams' first sizeable commissions in 1962. Teer and Spence report that:

> The message of the subsequent surveys were (sic) clear. For the first they were communicated to those who could benefit, not only the publicity group but also party officials and MP's. The first study was made up of interviews with 1,250 electors in marginal constituencies. The aim was to define the target voter in terms which the publicity group could use and MPs and officials could understand. And it was also to determine which issues were particularly pressing. The findings knocked on the head the original assumption made by Wilson in his 1955 report on party organisation that at least half the population were solidly Labour. They showed that the loyal supporters of the two major parties accounted for only about two-thirds of the electorate, that class, though important in defining which party a person supported, did not do so at all perfectly, that the uncommitted or floating voters were not drawn from any one particular section of the community, and that the vast majority of the voters were not ideological sophisticates and were not even particularly interested in politics. There were differences in the support given to certain 'policies' by Labour and Conservative backers but on many points where the Labour party did have a particular policy Labour and Conservative voters thought very similarly. The uncommitted voters differed from these in that they were not particularly keen on either party. The objectives for the advertisers were relatively clear. They were to concentrate

on the uncommitted voters, particularly in marginal seats, aiming
not only at the young but also at the old, at those with children
of school age and at the lower executive grades, most of whom
were not very interested in politics and policies. The survey did
not discover new policies, and was not intended to do so.

The survey research was continued in 1963 and 1964. Panels
of the uncommitted voters were sent questionnaires at regular
intervals and though several panels were kept going at the same
time to keep a check on the findings, and though response rates
did fall, continuing checks on those who did not reply showed
that they were not dissimilar to those who replied. The panel
findings were used to monitor advertising and to examine any
vital changes in the priorities of the voters. In 1963, for instance,
surveys found that Mr Wilson's popularity was greater than Mr
Macmillan's, as a result of which the propagandists turned the
spotlights on Mr Wilson.

Dr Abrams' reports were available and were reported to the
whole campaign committee, but remained confidential to the
campaign committee. One or two leaks apparently did occur,
for instance in May 1964 the *Daily Mail* reported: 'Labour's
investigations into public opinion show that the Tory campaign
on defence is beginning to have an effect − and that the time
has come to retaliate.' There are, however, those who believe
this 'leak' was inspired by those in Conservative Central Office
where emphasis on defence and foreign affairs was made in the
Conservative publicity campaign of the time. Survey research
was maintained even during the campaign itself in 1964 to
monitor public opinion of party political broadcasts, and the
overall result was clear. As Rose concluded: 'The 1964 Labour
publicity group demonstrated by its use of market research, by
its concentration upon the electoral audience and by the consist-
ency with which it emphasised a few messages, that a considerable, even though imperfect, degree of rationality could be
achieved in efforts to influence voters.'[3]

In 1967, ORC under Taylor began publishing regular
monthly polls in the *London Evening Standard*, also syndicated
in about 20 regional papers. In 1968, Marplan under Derek
Radford began publishing quarterly political surveys for *The
Times*, taken not only in Great Britain but in Northern Ireland
as well, and for regional newspapers. Later, first under John

Clemens and then Nicholas Sparrow, Marplan also published polls for the *Guardian* and for the Press Association and occasionally for the *Daily Express*. Originally set up in 1959 as a subsidiary of McCann Erickson Advertising Agency, Marplan was later sold to Unilever and then on to Ogilvy and Mather where in 1989, following a defection of its key directors, it quit polling altogether and later was closed; three of its directors, including Sparrow, left to set up ICM which now (1990) polls monthly for the *Guardian* newspaper.

There was also a brief appearance in the 1960s by Conrad Jamison and Associates (for the Labour party), A. J. Allen and Associates (for the *Guardian* and *The Economist*) and one or two others, none of whom had a continuing presence, except for Louis Harris Research Limited. This was an offshoot of the American firm then owned by Louis Harris himself, later by the Wall Street firm Donaldson, Lufkin, and subsequently by Gannet Newspapers. The Harris poll was first owned by a joint venture between Opinion Research Centre and Beaverbrook Newspapers, later to become Express Newspapers, and subsequently by Harris exclusively.

There were only two General Elections in the middle years, in 1964 and in 1966. During the period continuous polling was conducted by both Gallup and NOP, but at the 1964 election they were joined by the *Daily Express* poll (still not taken very seriously by either the paper or the public) and Research Services Limited under Mark Abrams, the Labour party's pollster, for the *Observer*. The methodology and reporting of details was very much improved by the middle years. NOP introduced a panel element, interviewing nearly 1,200 electors, all of whom had previously been interviewed unless they had been on holiday at the time of an earlier survey, and reporting in the *Mail* that 'A random sample was conducted among electors interviewed in all the four surveys that have been carried out since mid-September in 100 constituencies.'

The final Gallup surveys started on Thursday 8 October and finished on Tuesday 13 October, two days before election day. Gallup did one sample of 1,904 electors by quota sample and one random sample of 1,925 electors, totalling 3,829, on which they reported. The electoral share was two points lower for the Tories and two points higher for the Liberals, with Labour at 46% on both surveys.

The election was close, and the polls' record, on the whole, not bad (Table 2.1).

In 1964, as before and certainly since, share prices seemed to reflect poll stories, and were subject to hostile comment. Other publicity given to poll findings (especially in the by-elections) led to calls for banning them. In Orpington in 1962 the Liberal victory was widely thought to have been helped by publication of an NOP poll some ten days before polling day which indicated the likely possibility of toppling the Tory candidate if enough traditional Labour voters cast a 'tactical' vote for the Liberal. Resulting criticism seemed to enhance polls' reputation rather than detract from it. Butler and his King,[4] in their 1964 Nuffield series book, argued:

> Polling is after all only a systematic expansion of reporting. In a free society people must be allowed to enquire into and report on public opinion. A ban on the publication of polls would lead to a black market in rumour about the findings of private polls. The major remedy to any supposed evil caused by pre-election polls lies in lively and expert criticism of the polls' findings and in the growth of public understanding about the strengths and limitations of the polls. There is, in fact, no evidence whatever that opinion polls have ever induced bandwagon voting.
>
> Between September 17th and September 23rd the Gallup poll found that 38% of people claimed that they knew what at least one poll was showing. Gallup, which then showed Labour ahead, was thought by 15% to be doing so and by 11% to be showing the Conservatives in the lead; NOP which then showed the Conservatives ahead was thought by 15% to be doing so and by 7% to be showing Labour in the lead; the *Daily Express*, which then showed the Conservatives ahead, was thought by 11% to be doing so and by 6% to be showing Labour in the lead. This extraordinary level of inaccuracy in ordinary people's recall encourages scepticism about the potential of polls to create bandwagon effect.

According to Butler and King, 'Opinion polls reached a new level of political importance in the 1964 Parliament.

Table 2.1 General Election, 1964

Poll Newspaper	RSL Observer	NOP Daily Mail	Gallup Daily Telegraph	Own Daily Express	Actual result 15 Oct
Fieldwork	n/a	9–13 Oct	8–13 Oct	n/a	
Sample size	n/a	1,179	3,829	n/a	
	%	%	%	%	%
Con	45.0	44.3	44.5	44.5	42.9
Lab	46.0	47.4	46.5	43.7	44.8
Lib (+ others)	(9.0)	7.9	8.5	11.0	11.4
Others	0.0	0.4	0.5	0.8	0.9
Lab lead	+1.0	+3.1	+2.0	−0.8	+1.9
Error on lead	−0.9	1.2	0.1	1.1	(0.8)
Average error on share (+/−)	1.65	2.0	1.6	0.8	(1.5)
Maximum error	2.4	3.5	2.9	1.6	(2.6)

Everyone watching to see when Mr Wilson would decide to call an election knew that Mr Wilson was watching the polls.'

Some commentators also credited the polls with a critical influence on Sir Alec Douglas-Home's decision to give up the Conservative leadership. The influence of the polls was not dimmed by their vagaries, according to Butler and King, even though NOP came a 20% cropper on a by-election in January 1965, predicting a 20% win for Mr Patrick Gordon-Walker who, on the day, lost Leyton by half a per cent.

During the period there were also inexplicable differences between NOP and Gallup, but perhaps the most important impact was being made in Conservative Central Office by Humphrey Taylor, and in Transport House by Mark Abrams. A ringing endorsement of Taylor's work (he was engaged virtually full time on Tory work during the period) was made by one younger Central Office official who said: When old-timers talked nonsense before, all you could do was say 'Rubbish' and they'd just say 'Rubbish' back. Now you can produce some evidence.[5] It was important, too, that both Taylor and Abrams became known, principally through the *Sunday Times*, for their private polling for the parties.

By the 1966 election, the *Daily Telegraph*, *Daily Mail*, *Daily Express* and the *Observer* were joined by the *Guardian*, *Financial Times*, *The Economist* and the *Sunday Times* in publishing polls. The fact that the two most highly regarded polls agreed in showing Labour 10% or more ahead almost throughout the campaign took much of the steam out of the contest. This led to calls to ban polls, to which the defeated Mr Heath responded sharply: 'Ban polls? Of course not. You can't do that in a free society'; Mr Wilson, in an early Parliamentary reply as Prime Minister, flatly refused to consider any restriction on election polls.[6]

So, while the final polls (see Table 2.2) were within a reasonable distance of the result, apart from the *Express*, Research Services came out marginally closest, despite finishing fieldwork a week before polling day. NOP, alone among the polls, re-interviewed at the end of the campaign a sample of the people interviewed earlier, again using a panel technique for their

Table 2.2 General Election, 1966

Poll Newspaper'	RSL *Observer*	NOP *Daily Mail*	Own *Daily Express*	Gallup *Daily Telegraph*	Actual result 31 Mar
Fieldwork	n/a	27–29 Mar	n/a	24–28 Mar	
Sample size	n/a	1,693	n/a	3,596	
	%	%	%	%	%
Con	41.6	37.4	41.6	40.0	41.4
Lab	49.7	54.1	50.6	51.0	48.7
Lib (+ others)	(8.7)	7.5	(7.8)	8.0	8.8
Others	0.0	1.0	0.0	1.0	1.1
Lab lead	+8.1	+16.7	+9.0	+11.0	+7.3
Error on lead	+0.8	+9.4	+1.7	+3.7	(+3.9)
Average error on share (+/−)	0.8	2.7	1.4	1.2	(1.5)
Maximum error	1.2	5.4	1.9	2.3	(2.7)

prediction. Gallup once again used a huge sample, 2,019 random and 1,577 quota for a total sample of 3,596, on the basis that bigger must be better. It was not then and has not usually turned out to be, but the fact that they interviewed in more than 300 of the 630 constituencies shows how large an effort was made.

Butler and King concluded with a suggestion for the press and a warning for politicians:

> It is to be hoped that the press will now exploit the pollsters' techniques to throw light on opinion and attitudes in more sophisticated ways than hitherto. The Conservative party has belatedly found it worth while to invest considerable resources in the collection and analysis of survey data about the British public.
>
> If such research is not to be abused, it is desirable that the sort of information which parties may have at their disposal should also be gathered independently – and published.
>
> Politicians, and everyone else, can easily be misled by the apparent findings of polls. The intelligent statesman will neither ignore them nor be intimidated by them. In the short run public opinion sets limits to the politically possible and it is useful to know these limits. But public opinion can be fickle. As Winston Churchill showed before the war, there need be nothing suicidal in defying the opinion of the majority. It is worth remembering that democratic politicians have always conducted affairs with an eye on public opinion. They now have more accurate tools for measuring what public opinion really is. What they will need is education in how to use these tools – and how not to use them.[7]

The 1969 publication of *Political Change in Britain* by David Butler and Donald Stokes,[8] which analysed results from a panel study conducted in 1963, 1964 and 1966, had an important impact on politicians, journalists, political scientists and pollsters. Unfortunately, the much improved understanding of British electoral behaviour did not help the polls to an improved performance when the June 1970 General Election came along.

Notes

1 David Butler and Anthony King, *The British General Election of 1964* (Macmillan, 1965).
2 M. Abrams 'Opinion Polls and Party Propaganda', *Public Opinion Quarterly*, 28, no. 1, 1964, pp. 13–19.
3 Frank Teer and James Spence, *Political Opinion Polls* (Hutchinson University Library, 1973).
4 Butler and King, *General Election of 1964*.
5 (Dick Leonard), 'Poll Watcher Wanted', *The Economist*, 13 January 1979, p. 19.
6 Richard Hodder-Williams, *Public Opinion Polls and British Politics* (Routledge and Kegan Paul, 1970).
7 David Butler and Anthony King, *The British General Election of 1966* (Macmillan, 1966).
8 David Butler and Donald Stokes, *Political Change in Britain*, 2nd edn (Macmillan, 1968).

3 The General Election of 1970: Britain's 1948

During the 1970 election campaign there were five polls being published – the same number as in 1966 – but they were read by an enormously enhanced audience as exclusive publication was abandoned. Earlier, newspapers had jealously guarded the copyright they had on their polls. The result was that in 1970, when the polls got it so badly wrong, it was very much in the public eye.

For the first time, polls dominated campaign reporting; eight of the 23 issues of *The Times* published between 18 May and 18 June headlined poll results on the main front-page story. A Harris poll the following September found that 62% of the country remembered seeing polls (of those, 71% recalled seeing them on television). In the 'sunshine' election when the only surprise was the winner, polls dominated the election news.

ORC polled for the *Evening Standard* and the *Sunday Times*; Harris, the ORC off-shoot under Peter Bartram, whose first regular poll was in its founding year, 1969, polled for the *Daily Express*; Gallup for the *Daily Telegraph*, NOP for the *Daily Mail* and Marplan for *The Times*. ORC also continued its work for the Tories, together with a long-term panel study, fieldwork done by the British Market Research Bureau. Mark Abrams's departure meant that the *Observer* dropped Research Services and ran no poll and the Labour party began to use MORI, set up in 1969 by Robert Worcester as a joint venture between NOP and Opinion Research Corporation (USA).[1]

During the years between 1966 and 1970, public opinion, previously extraordinarily stable, began to swing more wildly. Labour, the 1966 victor, enjoyed a 20% lead in May 1966 but just two years later was 20% behind. Four years later, in May 1970 when the election was called, Labour was ahead again. In the midst of this, and following the polls' rather mediocre record in 1966, the Speaker's Conference on Electoral Law reported in June 1967, and recommended a 72-hour pre-election ban on the publication of poll findings. This recommendation was scorned by the press and leading politicians alike, and was not acted upon.[2]

The press reports of the polls during the period seldom gave interviewing dates, hardly ever reported 'don't knows' or refusals, seldom offered breakdowns of total results/top-line figures and showed little interest in issues. Sampling error was seldom mentioned, and headlines frequently screamed out shifts of electoral support based on statistically insignificant changes.

At the beginning of the 1970 campaign, however, led by Humphrey Taylor of ORC, the pollsters banded together (in self-defence) and published a Code of Practice which provided that the worst excesses of the papers would be curbed (see Appendix). The effect of the publication of the Code was to give the pollsters a weapon in their battles with their clients; for the most part, poll reports thereafter reported at least field-work dates, sample sizes and number of sampling points.[3]

In the event, after a notably wild month when NOP's trend-lines crossed Marplan's, ORC's crossed Harris's, and Gallup trends crossed themselves (one a national electorate series and the other taken in the marginals), they all got it wrong in straight poll figures (ORC adjusted its final figures by turnout to be on the right side, just, of a Tory victory). Harris tried hardest, combining a recall survey of 966 electors and a fresh sample of 1,184 electors in 32 selected marginal constituencies — but they did not get it right either (Table 3.1).

All published on election day, except Marplan who published a day earlier. NOP's final poll was based, as in 1964 and 1966, on re-interviews with some of the earlier samples to check on

Table 3.1 General Election, 1970

Poll	ORC	Harris	NOP	Gallup	Marplan	Actual result
Newspaper	London Standard	Daily Express	Daily Mail	Daily Telegraph	The Times	
Fieldwork	13–17 Jun	n/a	12–16 Jun	14–16 Jun	11–14 Jun	18 Jun
Sample Size	1,583	2,661	1,562	2,190	2,267	
	%	%	%	%	%	%
Con	46.5	46.0	44.1	42.0	41.5	46.2
Lab	45.5	48.0	48.2	49.0	50.2	43.8
Lib	6.5	5.0	6.4	7.5	7.0	7.6
Others	1.5	1.0	1.3	1.5	1.3	2.4
Lab lead	−1.0	+2.0	+4.1	+7.0	+8.7	−2.4
Error on lead	1.4	4.4	6.5	9.4	11.1	(6.6)
Average error on share (+/−)	1.0	2.1	2.2	2.6	3.2	(2.2)
Maximum error	1.7	4.2	4.4	5.2	6.4	(4.4)

Table 3.2   ORC's final prediction, 1970

	Survey 13–15 Jun (1,583)	Re-interviews 16–17 Jun (257)	Re-interviews adjusted for turnout
	%	%	%
Con	42.0	45.5	46.5
Lab	46.5	45.5	45.5
Lib/Others	11.5	9.0	8.0
Lab lead	+4.5	0	−1.0

change. Harris merged a 4% Labour lead in its final re-interview survey with a 1% Conservative lead in a special survey of marginals, finding a 3% Labour lead; then, making allowance for differential turnout, settled on a 2% labour forecast. ORC's forecast was based on a recall on 257 respondents interviewed earlier (recalls now being common practice), and corrected for differential turnout, as shown in Table 3.2. Only one voter ORC re-interviewed had switched from Conservative to Labour while 14 switched from Labour to Conservative and so on this thin reed ORC's reputation rested. Butler and Pinto-Duschinsky concluded: 'It is an ironic commentary 'on polls that if it had not been a final forecast and ORC had been following its normal routines, its headline on June 18 would have been 4% Labour lead, not a 1% Conservative lead.'[4]

Interestingly, in 1970 three polls had been conducted by random methods, two (ORC and Gallup) by quota. The mean error of random samples on the Conservative lead was 7.6, by quota samples, 5.4. NOP, Gallup and Marplan did not adjust their figures in any way (other than to reallocate 'don't knows'), ORC adjusted for differential turnout, as indicated above.

Why did the polls get it wrong? Late shifts and inaccurate quota sampling seemed to answer a similar question in the United States in 1948. Certainly the method of sampling did not appear to be the answer, and late shift evidence was suggestive rather than conclusive. Hypotheses were many, and included differential voting by non-contacts, organized deception on the part of Tory supporters, an anti-poll bandwagon, collusion on the part of the pollsters, selective turnout, and others. Post-mortems by the polls and academic examinations were for the most part inconclusive, but tended to support the late swing hypothesis.[5]

Public polls were in the limelight; private polls went underground. In the late 1960s and just into 1970 Mark Abrams had conducted the last of his work for the Labour party (on a budget of £15,000 according to Butler, £5,000 according to Abrams[6]), on a variety of subjects, including party activists, youth, party advertising and other topics. His last polling was done in the run-up to the 1970 General Election, and when he turned up in May to present the findings he was instructed not to distribute the 18 copies he had brought but to destroy them, which he did, except for the two copies he kept for his own records, still in his files.

It was just before then, in late 1969, that the party's and the Prime Minister's publicity advisers, David Kingsley, Peter Davis and Dennis Lyons, recommended that MORI be asked to do Labour's private polls. What follows in this book is my personal story of how MORI came to work with the Labour party in a relationship that has lasted over 20 years and six general elections. It is a story never before told, and it is to be hoped that someday the Conservative party's pollsters for even longer, ORC and its successor Harris, first Humphrey Taylor and then John Hanvey, will be able to reveal some of their history of private polling for the Tory party.

I had been working with a public relations consultant, Tim Traverse-Healy, on a survey of staff attitudes for the National Westminster bank. Tim's secretary Susan rang to ask me to come to lunch with Tim one day the following week. When I arrived at his office in Buckingham Gate, Susan explained that Tim was on a telephone call and would I like to meet his partner, Dennis Lyons, of whom I had not been aware before. I spent about 20 minutes with Dennis when Susan appeared, suggesting that we go on to lunch and that Tim would join us later. Later, over an hour later, Tim appeared at the restaurant. 'How are you two getting on?', he inquired. 'Fine,' said Dennis, who then turned to me and said 'How would you like to do the Prime Minister's polling?' That was the first inkling I had of the purpose of his many questions over the past hour and a half. He explained that he was one of the so-called 'three wise men' of the Wilson entourage, and that as Abrams was about to become a civil servant, they were casting about for someone who could and would do objective, professional research for the Prime Minister. They had had an abortive start with Conrad Jamison, who had been recommended to the group by one of the other 'wise men', David Kingsley, but he had not worked out, reportedly not finishing assignments to their satisfaction in the work that led to the 'Yesterday's Men' advertising campaign.

When I recovered from my astonishment, Dennis Lyons asked me to meet with his colleagues and with Percy Clark, the Labour party's publicity chief, at Peter Davis's house in Highgate, which I did in December 1969, after preparing an outline proposal for a programme of research for the anticipated 1970 General Election.

Like everyone else, MORI was instructed to plan for an autumn election and was startled (and unready) by the May election call. Only two studies were conducted: the first was a 2,000 case random survey to identify changers and potential changers, and on campaign issues. It identified working-class women, especially those living in the Midlands and the North, as the potential risk group, and prices as Labour's Achilles' heel. The party, for the most part unconcerned as a result of Mr Wilson's lead and the fine weather which promised a high turnout, none the less commissioned a second, quickie, poll on standards of living, Mr Wilson's (and Mr Heath's) television performance and canvassing.

Several aides, including Ron Hayward, then national agent and later to become Labour's General Secretary, sensed the message, especially that the public were fed up with the 'slanging' that the politicians were seen to be doing. Neither Hayward nor the party's pollster was invited to attend the top strategy meetings, but Hayward was sufficiently concerned to take the poll results to No. 10 to see Mr Wilson privately. His worries (and the poll's 2% Tory lead!) were dismissed by the Leader. Less than £10,000 was spent altogether, and there is no evidence that MORI had any impact on Labour's election strategy in 1970.[7] Nor was I told of any work being done by Abrams at the time.

The Conservatives, meanwhile, had mounted an elaborate and consistent programme of private polls. Starting in 1966, the Tories spent approximately £30,000 a year with ORC (and on the BMRB panel). There were continuous panel operations (starting with the 4,500 electors interviewed in 1965), re-interviewing 700 or so each seven months to detect and determine causes of changes in voting intentions. One startling finding was that at least 30% of the electorate had changed their voting intention in some way between 1964 and 1966, and these tended to be C2s (skilled working class), under-35s and women. This finding affected party policy, election strategy and advertising. It also brought a sense of proportion to Tory leaders, reminding them in the mid-term period when record anti-government swings both in the polls and in by-elections were running their way that the tide of public opinion went down as well as up.

The ORC work also included monthly studies on specific topics, issues, newspaper readership, critical seats etc. The findings from these were fed into Tory policy study groups as well as into Central Office and to the leadership. The sale of council houses, which proved to be such a winner for the Tories in 1979, was first discovered almost by accident in an ORC poll for the Greater London Council election in 1967 and first applied nationally – if gingerly – in 1970. Other work included polls the day after party broadcasts, publicity tests, slogan and semantic studies, speech impact studies and, of considerable importance, by-election studies.

The election campaign saw three sets of daily 'quickie' polls (with 500 respondents) on the previous night's television, on issues and on the impact of the mass media. These were telephoned back and ready by, respectively, lunchtime for the party's television advisers, tea-time for the Research department's issues team and early evening for the Central Office publicity people.

The contrast between the parties' polling operations has been likened to operating blind (Labour) and with 20−20 eyesight (Tories). In Transport House, polling figures were jealously guarded and available to a few; at Central Office they had a distribution list of over 50 and were regularly presented to the party leadership.

Notes

1   R. Rose, 'The Polls and the 1970 General Election', University of Strathclyde Survey Research Centre, Occasional Paper no. 7, 1970.
2   David Butler and Michael Pinto-Duschinsky, *The British General Election of 1970* (Macmillan, 1971).
3   Mark Abrams, 'The Opinion Polls and the 1970 British Election', *Public Opinion Quarterly*, vol. 34, no. 3, 1979, pp. 317−24.
4   Butler and Pinto-Duschinsky, *General Election of 1970.*
5   Market Research Society Committee on the Performance of the Polls, 'Public Opinion Polling on the 1970 Election', Market Research Society, 1972. 'The 1970 British Election'. Rose 'The 1970 General Election'.
6   Abrams, Letter to the author, 15 March 1990.
7   Butler and Pinto-Duschinsky, *General Election of 1970.*

4 The 1974 General Elections: Labour Squeaks Home

The period of the four years of Edward Heath's government was marked by its end in a futile attempt to curb the power of the trade unions, in an election marred by both its timing and its chosen theme. A badly prepared Labour party had only begun to mount its campaign team in mid 1973, its Leader having been surprised by his defeat in June 1970 and psychologically and financially unable to focus on much of anything but writing the book that would bring in sufficient funds for him and his staff to prepare for the coming election.

A key element in the Wilson preparation had been slotted into place in the summer of 1972, however, when Harry Nicholas, the lack-lustre General Secretary of the Labour party, was gracefully retired with his knighthood to make room for the promotion of Labour's wiry little national agent, Ron Hayward, to take over the helm at Transport House. Wilson also garnered funds from the Rowntree Trust to fund a team of research assistants, soon dubbed his 'chocolate soldiers', to assist in the preparation of the election strategy. Gwyn Morgan, the Assistant General Secretary, Terry Pitt, research director, and Tom McNally, international secretary, together with Hayward and his former assistant, Reg Underhill, now promoted to national agent, were the key in-house team. The Wilson personal entourage included Marcia Williams, later Lady Falkender, Joe Haines as press secretary, and general factotums Terry Boston, later Lord Boston, Albert Murray, later Lord Murray, and finally Dr Bernard Donoughue, later Lord Donoughue, who was originally brought into the team to liaise with the MORI people and their private polling findings. On the Tory side, Keith Britto was the insider at Central Office working with Humphrey Taylor and Tommy Thompson from ORC who provided the private polling for the Conservative campaign. These steps laid the groundwork for the election when it came.

The General Election of February 1974

An unspoken commentary on the record of the polls in 1970 is that for the first time since 1955 they did not receive a chapter to themselves in the Nuffield book on the election.[1] Despite this, in 1974 the polls were as much quoted in the press and perhaps even more on television as they were in 1970, and both major parties mounted substantial private polling programmes.

Six polling organizations conducted major national polls for the press. All contracts continued except that *The Times* dropped Marplan in favour of ORC and the *Observer* re-entered the polling business with Business Decisions, then part owned by Gallup. From the outset the polls presented a confused picture. Gallup, ORC and Harris all published Conservative leads on St Valentine's Day, two weeks before election day, of 1.5%, 2% and 11% (sic) respectively. Earlier, Marplan (for ITV's *Weekend World*) had shown a 6% Tory lead while Business Decisions' (*Observer*) poll showed a 7.7% Conservative lead on 10 February. The polls plainly had an impact on the Liberals, according to Butler and Kavanagh.[2]

After an early slump, every poll showed a trend to the Liberals, which gave added impetus to the Liberal bandwagon. It was an unpopular election – the result of a confrontation between the miners (who had great sympathy among the public) and Edward Heath (who had respect but little sympathy). Mr Heath's pollster, still the now-familiar Humphrey Taylor, urged a quick, sharp election in January. He presented his findings on Friday 11 January and according to the account of Mr Heath's then political secretary, now Foreign Secretary Douglas Hurd, 'Taylor, in particular, had a strong hold on our judgements because they alone had predicted victory in 1970. The evidence of his surveys was not conclusive, but Humphrey Taylor in his exposition deduced that we should win an early election'. Taylor also stated at that time that "the tide would slip away".[3]

Hurd agreed with the Taylor analysis, as a manuscript note he wrote to Mr Heath on 15 January showed: 'The result of the election would depend on whether the deep dislike of trade union militancy which the research reveals ... is stronger that the unpopularity of the Government. I agree with Humphrey Taylor et al that it is stronger at present, but will not remain so.'

Thus Taylor's advice was considered, but Mr Heath soldiered on while Labour frantically prepared their attack. The effect of the month's delay was to throw away the key advantage of surprise that a British Prime Minister enjoys of a nearly sole right to determine when an election shall be (only in practice otherwise subject to a five-year limit on the life of a Parliament or the loss of a vote of confidence in the House of Commons).

The Tory government was generally agreed to have won the first week's campaign on the theme of 'Who runs Britain?', but by the second, Labour's concerted attack on the government's handling of the economy began to turn the tide. One hopeful Conservative party official propounded a 'V-shaped theory of voting behaviour': 'The Government always wins the first week. The Opposition always gains in the second week. The big question is how near the Government comes to regaining the peak of the first week.'[4] It did not.

On the day, the published polls were close, but too Tory. The Labour party's private poll findings, conducted by MORI, which showed a 1% Conservative lead, were leaked to the *Daily Mirror* 'in the hope that this would mobilise voters'.[5] The Conservatives won the popular vote, by 0.8%, but Labour, with more MPs elected, won the election (see Table 4.1).

The two employing the largest sample sizes, random sampling

Table 4.1 General Election, February 1974

Poll Newspaper	Bus. Dec. *Observer*	ORC *London Standard*	Harris *Daily Express*	NOP *Daily Mail*	Gallup *Daily Telegraph*	Marplan *Ldn Wknd Television*	Actual result
Fieldwork	21 Feb	n/a	26–27 Feb	23–27 Feb	26–27 Feb	n/a	28 Feb
Sample size	1,056	2,327	3,193	4,038	1,881	1,649	
	%	%	%	%	%	%	%
Con	36.0	39.7	40.2	39.5	39.5	36.5	38.8
Lab	37.5	36.7	35.2	35.5	37.5	34.5	38.0
Lib	23.0	21.2	22.0	22.0	20.5	25.0	19.8
Others	3.5	2.4	2.6	3.0	2.5	4.0	3.4
Labour lead	+1.5	−3.0	−5.0	−4.0	−2.0	−2.0	−0.8
Error on lead	−2.3	−2.2	−4.2	−3.2	−1.2	−1.2	(2.4)
Average error on share (+/−)	1.7	1.2	1.8	1.5	0.7	2.9	(1.6)
Maximum error	3.2	1.4	2.8	2.5	0.9	5.2	(2.7)

and re-interviewing, Harris and NOP, were the furthest adrift. The closest published poll, Gallup, used a quota sample of 1,013 and a re-interview of 868 respondents. All were using belt-and-braces tactics after their 1970 fiasco. Yet the poll that came closest, the Labour party's private MORI poll, used a quota sample of fewer than a thousand respondents, the field-work being on the Tuesday before polling day.

The ORC–Harris people were quick to cry *mea culpa*. ORC's private polls had indicated the Tories would coast in. Mr Louis Harris was in Britain and both on television and in the *Daily Express* said: 'We ... could not have been more mistaken.' Taylor told *The Times*: 'We very much regret that we misled a great many people into believing the Conservatives would win by a comfortable majority', and T. F. (Tommy) Thompson, ORC Chairman, said: 'Once again the opinion polls as a whole appear to have misled commentators, the public and the poli-ticians themselves.' Yet all polls said the Tories would get more votes than Labour – and they did.

All the polls overestimated the Liberals – who did not contest 106 seats and the pollsters failed to take this into account. All the polls underestimated Labour – all but Marplan adjusted for differential turnout and in each instance this increased the Tory lead erroneously.[6] And the difficulty of translating votes, which is what the polls measure, into seats in the House of Commons, this time was crucial. Rose,[7] in *Britain at the Polls*, discussed the problem at length. Rose concluded his treatise on the polls and the February 1974 election with the following thoughtful remarks:

> The 1974 election demonstrated that newspapers are not interested in using the polls to do anything more than give a forecast about which party is winning or will win the election. The *Daily Mail* and the *Daily Express* consistently gave the scantiest of details about what was in the minds of the voters: one question and one question only, voting intention, concerned these newspapers. The scanty coverage is particularly striking in that although the *Mail* and the *Express* spent more money on high quality samples than any other paper, they neglected to publicise in detail what their money bought, or even to give briefly the technical facts documenting the quality of their

samples. After the election, both polls issued on their own account well-documented studies reporting more details of their pre-election polls than their client newspapers wished to print. The serious papers, with smaller type and much more lineage, gave more space to reporting the opinions of voters; but first priority was always given to opinions that voters would tend to corroborate or qualify the replies about voting intentions – for example, attitudes about party leaders or about which party would handle best the most important questions of the day.

The single-mindedness of the press is striking because the British press was burnt in 1970 by publicizing election forecasts that were wrong by any standard. This single-mindedness is also surprising because the 1974 election occurred at a time when the issues facing the country were very serious and popular attitudes uncertain. Yet no paper during the campaign used opinion poll data to explore in depth the reaction of the British people to a domestic crisis as grave as any in a generation.

The chief conclusion that this writer would draw from the performance of the polls (and the press) is that there is need for fundamental rethinking about polls by those who sponsor them. Each newspaper editor currently sponsoring a poll should ask himself a simple question: Why am I doing this? If it is 'to get tomorrow's news today', he should realize that the risks of getting the story wrong are real, especially at a time when the party system and the electoral system are not working as predictably as in the quarter-century since 1945.

Ironically, the press could provide more political information for its readers if it returned to the original concept of the polls as a device for assessing opinion, rather than for forecasting behaviour. An error margin of 3 or 5 percentage points is of little consequence if one wishes to ascertain how the country divides on matters of policy, or abortion. It is technically simple (and economically attractive) to take the results of a single poll and use them in several different stories reporting popular attitudes about issues of the day. In fact, before the surge of interest in forecasting polls, the now defunct *News Chronicle* published brief stories several times a week giving Gallup Poll reports of popular opinions about issues without regard to voting intention.

This was the first General Election campaign in which both major parties had invested in extensive pre-election and daily election polls. It was the first time polls were described as 'a permanent part of the parties' campaign armoury'.[8] It was the first time both parties' pollsters sat at the 'top table' and it was the first extensive use of psychographic/values research and of multivariate analysis of large-scale panel data (by MORI, for the Labour party).

ORC had been conducting regular polls on issues, target voters, and the like, but had neither the budget nor the attention they enjoyed while the Conservatives were out of office in the 1966–7 period. The nature of British politics is that the focus of political leaders in power is, naturally enough, the running of the government, while, again naturally enough, the focus of the 'outs' is getting back. This tends both to loosen party purse strings and 'concentrate the mind wonderfully' on anything which may assist in winning back the reins of government.

This, no doubt, was a factor in the Labour party's decision in July 1972 to employ MORI on a regular basis, both to advise and interpret published polls and to carry out extensive qualitative and quantitative research on behalf of the party. In addition to a large-scale panel study, several by-election studies and run-up tracking studies, MORI published a monthly Public Opinion Digest from late 1972 through to the autumn of 1974, initially in 50 copies to the party's Campaign Committee and senior Transport House staff and eventually 2,000 copies sent to all local constituency parties, all Labour MPs and parliamentary candidates, all professional staff and others.

The private research carried out during this period and during the election was closely guarded, although presented internally to such groups in addition to the Campaign Committee as the regional organizers, research department staff, the national executive of Young Socialists and party advertising advisers.

In the autumn of 1973, a small team consisting of the late Percy Clark, publicity director of the party, Dennis Lyons (the late Lord Lyons), Peter Davis (later Lord Lovell-Davis) and Dr Bernard Donoughue, lecturer at LSE, joined together (assisted by Adrian Shaw, one of Mr Wilson's staff aides) to work with MORI on the formulation of questions for a series of semi-monthly, 2,000-case tracking studies to consider poll findings and advise Mr Wilson on pre-campaign tactics. This group met weekly, and their work enabled the party to be up-to-date on public attitudes to issues as it had never been before. It also worked out a planned programme of research focusing on attitudes of key identified target segmentations in the electorate, and honed the group of a fine edge that enabled them to work closely and well together when the election finally came.

The research was driven by a voting behaviour model of the British electorate (Figure 4.1) which began with the individual elector and attempted to measure the effect of demographics, geography, parental voting behaviour and past voting behaviour as a 'state of mind' at the point a General Election is called. Then, to measure 'environmental' considerations (at a time when the word 'environmental' had entirely different connotations than it does today), e.g. an individual elector's attitudes to the state of the economy, Britain's role in the world, the social environment, the local environment and the influences of family/peers etc.

These considerations were then influenced (or not) by political party considerations such as the elector's perception of the party's policies, personalities, local issues, their knowledge and image of the local MP, of the Prime Minister and other party considerations leading to a state of mind (I) that was either unexposed or influenced by the media channels of communications, including TV, party political broadcasts, national and local newspapers, hoardings, opinions by the local Member and being canvassed.

These influences led to a state of mind (II) which led the elector to make a decision to vote or not based on the various influences relating to that decision and, finally, the determination to which party to vote for or which to avoid.

The false election period in January 1974 intensified the group's efforts and when the election call came a final panel recall was initiated, a series of daily 'quickie' surveys was launched and a special sounding was taken in Scotland (MORI liaised with a separate Scottish group on this work).

The daily polls were based on 540 interviews using a tightly

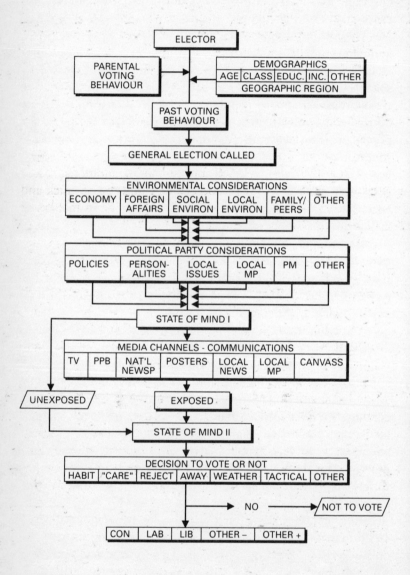

Figure 4.1 Voter model used for MORI polling programme for the Labour party, 1973−79

controlled interlocking (18-cell) quota sample in 54 randomly selected constituencies throughout Britain. Their questionnaire coverage was mixed, voting intention being used mainly for cross-analysis (the figures themselves were given only to Mr Wilson and General Secretary Ron Hayward after early, and damaging, leaks occurred). The questionnaires were short, usually about ten questions. Among the key topics were issues, salience and party preference, canvassing, television broadcast recall and assessment, 'slanging', 'promises the country cannot afford' and national press readership (for cross-analysis purposes). A pattern of questions was worked out in advance with some questions asked daily, some every other day and many less frequently. Space was left for last-minute additions. These polls were used by the party to keep its campaign on track and were used principally (as were the Tories' polls) in matters of tactics and presentation of policy.

A last-minute addition to the polling programme was a 1,000-case Scottish sample, as the rise in the Scottish National Party's support placed a number of Scottish Labour seats in jeopardy. The strategy had to be 'hold Scotland and Wales, and get gains in England'. The results of the Scottish surveys determined shifts in the party's stance, helped shape Mr Wilson's key Glasgow speech, and was thought by some to be an important factor in Labour's relative success in Scotland.

Computers have added greatly to the ability of pollsters to analyse data and draw conclusions. Data can be weighted using complex multicellular calculations all interrelated. Cross-tabulation, automatic mean-score calculations, standard deviation and other statistical tests can be accomplished easily and quickly. And some use has been made of fairly complex multivariate analysis schemes, even in the pressure of a three-week election period.

In the private polling for the Labour party in the February 1974 General Election, a panel study was used to measure not only aggregate shifts in public opinion, which was mainly done with the small-scale samples of the electorate described above to get quick, daily, snapshots of reactions to party election broadcasts, leaders' speeches etc., but to measure individual change, and probe reasons for change in extensive open-ended questioning. The panel was also used to obtain measures of salience of issues, party identification with these issues, and the respondent's own position on each. In addition, extensive questioning was conducted about party image.

This data base provided the information that was used in multivariate computer analyses, both factor analysis and cluster analysis, to identify which groups of potential voters could be moved by better understanding the Labour party's policies where they were consonant with the voters' own views, and which image attributes were key to moving the identified groups towards Labour.

My confidential memorandum summarizing the report to the Prime Minister, Harold Wilson, and his entourage is reproduced in full below.[9]

Polls Group –

The analysis of the panel data on the model has shown several important and disturbing findings.

1 *Cluster I* – Committed Labour ('Old Fred'): 20% have deserted Labour, many (8%) won't vote.
2 *Cluster II* – Committed Labour ('Jack'): 11% have deserted Labour, most (8%) to Liberal.
3 *Cluster VI* – Floating Left: Labour has lost 19%, 13% have gone to the Liberals (22% of the Liberals' support comes from this group).
4 *Cluster VII* – Floating Right: Labour has lost 12%, Tories 8%. There were *no* Liberals in 1973 in this group. Now there are 24%.
5 *Cluster IV* – Apathetic: Labour has lost 8%, Liberals have gone from 6% of this group to 25%, although it is still unlikely these people will actually vote – *and they represent 37% of the Liberals' vote!*

So what?

1 'Committed' Labour voters (I) are most concerned with *house prices* and *mortgages* and *taxes* and if brought back to 1973 levels could mean 2%

2 'Committed' Labour voters (II) are most concerned with *wages* and *salaries* and *poverty* and could mean 2%

3 'Floating Left', if brought back from the Liberals on the issues of *unemployment, poverty, wages* and *salaries*, and if the Party can convince them they *keep their promises* and *represent all classes*, could be 4%

4 'Floating Right' is better left taking votes from Tories to Liberal 0%

5 'Apathetic' group, less likely to vote, taking votes to Liberal from Tories at twice the rate as Labour, still can contribute if convinced on *house prices* and strikes, to the tune of 1%

TARGET 9%

Nine per cent of an 80% turnout represents nearly 3,000,000 votes and dozens of seats. In the time that remains can we stress that the Labour Party *keeps its primises* and *represents all classes*, and can solve the problem of:

1 Wages and salaries
2 House prices
3 Poverty
4 Unemployment

The Labour Party has turned the main issue of the campaign from 'Who Runs Britain' to Cost of Living, LP spokesmen have cut out the slanging — Bob Mellish and the young candidates put a positive programme across — in the week that's left the research would suggest the maximum impact could be made by using the above strategy.

The findings from these studies and those of the October 1974 General Election were lodged by direction of the National Executive Committee of the Labour party at the SSRC Archives at the University of Essex, but embargoed until after the 'next' (May 1979) election.

Former Prime Minister (then Sir, now Lord) Harold Wilson commented on MORI's work for the Labour party in his prcsidential address to the Market Research Society's 1978 Conference:

> It is no secret that Bob Worcester and MORI produced daily polls for me in the most speculative of all elections, the 'confrontation' election of 1974, when even the most experienced politician could not forecast whether it would be confined to a single issue − where we might have lost − or whether my effort to widen it would succeed. At the end of the day, we had a plurality of five seats, with, for the first time, the arrival of considerable numbers of MPs from new parties. What Bob Worcester's polls were so useful for, and it was to this that they were directed, was the highlighting of issues. A political leader in a general election, apart from being chronically overworked and unable to study even the daily press very carefully, is like a warrior or a pilot operating in almost total fog.
>
> What we got − and I have no doubt our opponents had the same − were authoritative estimates on public opinion on which were the most important issues. Was it simply 'who runs the country − the Government or the miners'? Or was the Common Market a big issue? What about the cost of living − or housing? Were pensions a big issue? How were different groups of the nation, constituency, regions, age groups going to vote on some of these big issues? What difference would nationalisation make? What were the Liberals doing and where?
>
> This was more important by far than daily estimates of the total final vote. On this latter question, I am an agnostic, though not an atheist. I could be convinced, but on the identification of issues I believe market research has a valuable role to play provided that, as in any other campaign, intelligence is the servant and never the master of those conducting the campaign. So much depends on hunch and long years of training − and knowing people and their areas.
>
> And of course, as political market research has become more sophisticated, those responsible are more able not only to recognise the limitations of their research, but also to make allowance for the underlying factors.[10]

The General Election of October 1974

Polls regained their own chapter in the October 1974 Nuffield book,[11] despite the egg on their face. Every single prediction in

June 1970 had been too Labour, every single prediction in February 1974 was too favourable to the Conservatives. The pollsters were on the defensive.

Client—poll liaisons were largely unchanged. As in February, ORC was used by *The Times, London Evening Standard* and the Conservative party. Marplan (whose 1970 forecast in *The Times* was the worst General Election forecast ever recorded in Britain) was working for the 'popular' Murdoch papers (the *Sun* and the Sunday *News of the World*). Gallup polled for the *Daily Telegraph*, Harris for the *Daily Express* and NOP for the *Daily Mail*, although it produced no final predictive poll. Harris had also replaced Marplan for *Weekend World* on Independent Television. Business Decisions carried on for the *Observer* and ORC conducted a limited panel operation for the *Sunday Times*. During the three-week election campaign the published polls carried out some 40,000 interviews with well over 10,000 more conducted privately.

Every poll apart from one (NOP, 16 September) showed Labour comfortably ahead. The polls were also published in a more clustered way than ever before. Of the 25 polls that were published, 20 appeared on a Thursday or a Sunday, none on a Monday or Tuesday and only one on a Friday or Saturday. During the last week there were no polls on the Monday and Tuesday before polling despite numerous City rumours to the contrary. Then when the *Daily Mail* published an NOP poll on Wednesday, 9 October, showing a 14.5% Labour lead (fieldwork 2—5 October), followed on election day, Thursday, by Marplan with 10.5% Labour, Harris, 8.4% Labour, ORC, 7.4% Labour and Gallup, 5.5% Labour, only the fact that they had got it so wrong before kept interest alive. In the event, they were mostly wrong again, this time too Labour, and pro-government (see Table 4.2).

NOP and the *Daily Mail* stated their eve-of-poll result was not intended as a forecast. It was, however, widely considered to be such. It showed a 14.5 Labour lead. NOP and Harris employed random sampling (combined sample of over 4,000) and overestimated Labour's lead by 7%; Gallup, ORC and Marplan used quota samples re-interviewed and were out 7.8%. All used late fieldwork, re-interviews and adjustment for turnout (save Gallup), but all (save Gallup and Business Decisions, with fieldwork over a week before polling day) were outside the plus or minus 2/3% deemed acceptable. Other theories having fallen by the wayside, there followed the observation that the October 1974 election was the fourth in a row in which every single poll overestimated the support for the party that was in the lead. This led to the speculation of the 'underdog' effect, replacing the 'bandwagon' effect that had held sway earlier. Of course the May 1979 results negated that theory, with three under- and two overestimating the Tory share and all within ±2%.

Turnout adjustments this time (they usually favour the Tories) improved predictions: ORC reduced a 10% lead to 7.4%, Harris reduced an 11% Labour lead to 8.4%. Marplan did not ask a question about likelihood of voting in its *Sun* survey.

According to Butler and Kavanagh,[12] the two main parties' private polls' programmes were similar. ORC augmented its February research design by adding advertising effectiveness studies and especially focusing on the possibility of a Liberal breakthrough. Labour had MORI continue its fortnightly 2,000-case tracking studies in the summer, and two 1,000-case studies of substantial length mounted in Scotland, some motivational research and another recall on the 1973 panel. Its election period effort was expanded from the February model, with all broadcasts, including the Liberals', being measured.

The value of private polls is often challenged by party officials, sometimes on the grounds that they duplicate much that is available from published sources. Yet that they offer a quick, focused, and confidential assessment of specific campaign problems was certainly proved in this election. On Friday 27 September, when Mrs Thatcher, then a Shadow Minister, announced a policy of 9.5% mortgages and guaranteed to implement the Tory mortgage promise 'by Christmas', her promise received widespread coverage on television and in the weekend's newspapers. This worried the Labour party, and tentative plans were made to counter the offer. A MORI survey on the Sunday, however, found that 63% of the public felt the Conservatives were 'making promises the country cannot

Table 4.2 General Election, October 1974

Poll	Bus.Dec.	NOP	ORC	Harris	Gallup	Marplan	Actual result
Newspaper	Observer	Daily Mail	London Standard	Daily Express	Daily Telegraph	Sun	
Fieldwork	2 Oct	2–5 Oct	5–9 Oct	5–9 Oct	3–8 Oct	8 Oct	10 Oct
Sample sizes	2,071	1,978	1,071	2,701	954	1,024	
	%	%	%	%	%	%	%
Con	35.5	31.0	34.4	34.6	36.0	38.3	36.7
Lab	40.0	45.5	41.8	43.0	41.5	43.8	40.2
Lib	20.0	19.5	19.4	19.3	19.0	19.5	18.8
Others	4.5	4.0	4.4	3.1	3.5	3.5	4.3
Lab lead	+4.5	+14.5	7.4	+8.4	+5.5	+10.5	+3.5
Error on lead	+1.0	+11.0	3.9	+4.9	+2.0	+7.0	(5.0)
Average error on share (+/−)	0.7	3.0	1.2	1.6	+0.8	2.1	(1.6)
Maximum error	1.2	5.7	2.3	2.8	+1.3	3.6	(2.8)

afford', compared to 45% who thought so on the previous Thursday, the day before Mrs Thatcher's promise. This settled the issue for Labour; Conservative private polls later showed that less than half the electorate believed the 9.5% pledge.

Butler and Kavanagh report that the private polls for both parties, ORC for the Tories and MORI for Labour, stayed fairly stable throughout the campaign with a comfortable Labour lead until the end when both reported to their clients a Conservative advance in the final few days. The report on my final memorandum, written on 9 October, the day before the election, forecast a 2.5% swing to Labour, a 40 majority over the Conservatives and a five- to ten-seat overall majority. The final result was a 2.2% swing to Labour, a 43-seat Labour majority over the Tories, and an overall majority of three seats.

Shifting electoral intentions, obscured by independent surveys, continued to be identified by panel studies. In October 1974, Harris found that 23% of their panel respondents changed their voting intentions between dissolution and election day while 33% of the smaller ORC/*Sunday Times* panel reported that they had changed their minds, less than the 43% they had found in February but much more than the 20% recorded in comparable studies a decade earlier.

Further, recall studies conducted by NOP after each 1974 campaign showed that while two-thirds of the electorate claimed to have made up their minds before the election was called, there was still a victory to be fought for, and an election to be won, or lost, during the three-week campaign.

The European Referendum: 1975

The long period between October 1974 and April 1979, when Parliament forced an election on a reluctant Prime Minister, was enlivened by Britain's first national referendum (on the EEC), a devolution referendum in Scotland, the resignation of Harold Wilson and the election of Jim Callaghan as Leader of the Parliamentary Labour Party and thereby Prime Minister, and the reportedly 'accidental' election of Margaret Thatcher

Table 4.3 EEC Referendum, 1975

	Gallup	ORC	Harris	Marplan	NOP	MORI	Actual result
	%	%	%	%	%	%	%
Yes	68	73.7	72	68	68	67	67
No	32	26.3	28	32	32	33	33
Yes lead	36	47.4	44	36	36	34	34
Error on lead	+2	+13.4	+10	+2	+2	0	(4.9)

to replace Edward Heath as Tory Leader. It was also a period of minority government, when the Liberals (formally) and other parties in practice kept a cautious Labour party in power.

The EEC Referendum, in June 1975, gave the polls their first chance to measure their skills against an outcome in Britain that did not have to be translated into seats in the House of Commons. On the whole, they came out very well, although, once again, the random sample (Harris) performed worse, not better, than quota ones, and larger sample sizes did not necessarily mean better (Table 4.3, p. 59).

Four of the results were as close as anyone can get, but as Butler and Kitzinger[13] observed: 'The error in the forecast of ORC (13% in terms of the gap between victor and vanquished) was greater than in any final poll in any British general election since 1945.'

Notes

1 David Butler and Dennis Kavanagh, *The British General Election of February 1974* (Macmillan, 1974).

2 Ibid.

3 Douglas Hurd, *An End to Promises: Sketch of a Government 1970–1974*.

4 Robert M. Worcester, 'Winning in the Rain', *New Society*, 31, no. 643, 13 February 1975, p. 394.

5 Butler and Kavanagh, *February 1974*.

6 Ivor Crewe, et al., 'The Why and How of Voting in February 1974', in R. Rose (ed.), *Studies in British Politics*, 3rd edn (Macmillan, 1976), pp. 239–53.

7 Richard Rose, 'The Polls and Election Forecasting in February 1974 and the Polls and Public Opinion in October 1974', in H. Penniman (ed.), *Britain at the Polls* (American Enterprise Institute, Washington, DC, 1974), pp. 109–30, 223–39.

8 Butler and Kavanagh, *February 1974*.

9 Robert M. Worcester and Hon. Angela Mais, 'Campaign Polling Presentation', Confidential Research Studies conducted for the Labour Party, Market & Opinion Research International, 5 March 1974.

10 Sir Harold Wilson, 'Market Research in the Private and Public Sectors', *Journal of the Market Research Society*, 20, no. 3, July 1978, pp. 111–26.

11 Butler and Kavanagh, *The British General Election of October 1974* (Macmillan, 1975).

12 Butler and Kavanagh, *October 1974*.

13 David Butler and Uwe Kitzinger, *1975 Referendum* (Macmillan), p. 251.

Part II
Political Opinion Polling in the First Thatcher Decade: 1979–1989

5 The 1979 General Election: Political Watershed

When the election finally did come it was long expected, and most polling contracts had been long set. Gallup had continued its every-third-Thursday time-series in the *Telegraph*, and swung into the election without a pause. NOP, owned by the Daily Mail Group, had published sporadically only under a somewhat strained relationship with the *Mail's* editor, and Marplan continued with the *Sun*, which had eclipsed the Daily Mirror as Britain's best selling newspaper. The main change was that following Humphrey Taylor's move to the United States to work with Louis Harris in 1976, the editor of the *Sunday Times* Harold Evans retained MORI. Then the *Evening Standard*'s editor Charles Wintour, together with his shrewd political editor, the late Robert Carvel, an avowed admired of Taylor, brought the polling contract for the Express Group (*London Evening Standard* and *Daily Express*) to MORI as well. The next year MORI was approached by another Taylor client, the *Scotsman*, and asked to do their polling also.

ORC continued to do the Tories' private polling under its new managing director and long-time Taylor associate John Hanvey, and Labour continued to employ MORI. Research Services returned to political polling (under new people and after a decade) for the *Observer*.

The use sponsors make of polls is neatly, if perhaps too simply, summed up by Butler and Kavanagh: 'In a general election the press sponsors public opinion polls which are concerned with predicting the result; the parties sponsor private opinion polls which are concerned with analysing reactions to the campaign.'[1] There were more published polls than ever before. The reason for this was that the campaign was a long one, by design in part and partially to give the public their Easter long weekend. Again, some 50,000 electors were questioned about their voting intention and other matters by the major polling organizations.

From the outset, the Conservatives led by a substantial margin, but nothing like the 21% recorded by RSL in the *Observer* on the first Sunday of the campaign. Advised by Tony King, their first poll departed from the usual practice of asking those who refuse or say 'they don't know' how they will vote with a follow-up question such as 'which party are you more inclined to support?' or 'which party do you lean towards?'. In an effort to bring their obviously errant findings into line, later surveys revised the questioning procedure, although this did not bring their polls into accord with the others. Most commentators quickly cautioned reading much into the RSL findings, although they were duly included in the 'poll of polls' calculated by several newspapers.

Leaving RSL aside, the message of the polls throughout the campaign was clear: 15 out of 15 polls taken between the call of the election and 25 April, i.e. over the first three weeks of the campaign, had the Tories at 48% + 2% and Labour at 40% + 2%. The fourth week of the campaign, sensing a handsome Tory victory, the public narrowed the gap, first in MORI's poll in the Saturday's *Daily Express* reporting a 3% Tory lead, then in the NOP 0.7% Labour lead reported on TV on the Monday evening before polling day and published in the *Daily Mail* on the Tuesday. Asked that day by a journalist if I was a 'bandwagon' or a 'boomerang' man, I said: 'In this election I'd say I'm a 'boomerang-backlash-bandwagon' man.' By that I meant that the public were then boomeranging against the thought of an 80–100-seat Tory majority, but would back-lash when they thought Labour might win after all, and in the final day or two of the campaign would bandwagon as the momentum of the backlash built up. In the event, I think that is exactly what happened.

On the day, the polls proved to be nearly all within a whisker of the actual result (Table 5.1). Gallup, closest in both 1974 elections, was furthest out, yet still in terms of average error well within the normal sampling limits of $+/-2\%$ given their substantial sample, although considerably overestimating the Labour share. The polls with the latest fieldwork, NOP and MORI, neatly bracketed the gap, within a single percentage point, between both the Labour and Liberal share of vote.

In contradiction to the earlier Butler–Kavanagh quotation, the *Sunday Times*, alas on strike during the campaign, none the less commissioned MORI to conduct the most extensive evaluative survey research programme sponsored by a newspaper to date. In 1976, when the *Sunday Times*' political team and MORI agreed the panel outline, it was determined that the study's purpose was to be explanatory rather than predictive, and that its objective would be to explain, throughout the campaign and following its conclusion on election day, why what happened did happen and who among the electorate was affected by the campaign itself.

Two reasons were behind this decision: one, the fact that there is substantial evidence to indicate that in the last three General Elections preceding this one the election was won and/or lost in the last week of the campaign and therefore that the publication of data necessarily collected nearly a week before election day precluded a predictive effort; second, that the nature of the *Sunday Times* itself is one of 'insight' and analysis, and thus a panel study, with its unique ability to examine with absolute precision whether an individual's voting intention had indeed changed between week one in the election and, say, week three, because MORI were recalling on the same people throughout and immediately following the campaign, would provide a sounder analytical tool.

Of course any panel study introduces bias into the attitudes and behaviour of its members. Also it is recognized that the nature of a recall survey means that some of its original members are unable to be contacted in later weeks due to illness, holidays,

Table 5.1 General Election, May 1979

Poll Newspaper	Gallup Daily Telegraph	MORI Daily Express	Marplan Sun	NOP Daily Mail	MORI London Standard	Actual result
May Fieldwork	30 Apr–1 May	30 Apr–1 May	1 May	1–2 May	2 May	3 May
Sample size	2,348	974	1,973	1,069	1,089	
	%	%	%	%	%	%
Con	43.0	44.4	45.0	46.0	45.0	44.9
Lab	41.0	38.8	38.5	39.0	37.0	37.7
Lib	13.5	13.5	13.5	12.5	15.0	14.1
Other	2.5	3.3	3.0	2.5	3.0	3.3
Con lead	2.0	5.6	6.5	7.0	8.0	7.2
Error on lead	−5.2	−1.6	−0.7	−0.2	+0.8	(1.7)
Average error on share (+/−)	1.6	0.6	0.5	1.2	0.5	(0.9)
Maximum error	3.4	1.1	0.8	1.3	0.9	(1.5)

Table 5.2   General Election, 1979: MORI/*Sunday Times* panel results

Week	1	2	3	4
Dates	4–6 Apr	17–19 Apr	24–26 Apr	1–5 May
Sample size	1,087	928	894	883
% of original	100	85	82	81

Source: MORI/*Sunday Times* panel

lack of patience. In this instance, a reasonable recall rate was achieved (as indicated in Table 5.2) and in each case the recall sample was weighted in the computer analysis to ensure that a differential recall achievement (say between young people and OAPs) did not affect the analysis.

The findings

At the General Election on 3 May 1979, 92% of the panel members voted, according to the results of the recall survey conducted on the Friday and Saturday, 4–5 May, following election day. As the actual turnout was only 76%, it is likely that the experience of being interviewed repeatedly throughout the campaign had the effect of heightening interest in the campaign and increasing turnout. It did not, however, much affect voting behaviour, other than slightly to overstate the Conservative and Labour party shares and understate the Liberal vote somewhat. One interesting finding of the panel study is that two-thirds (65%) of those who said they would not vote did so on the day. Another is that nearly a quarter (24%) of the electorate changed their mind (at least once) during the course of the campaign.

The published polls had shown that there was very little change during the first three weeks of the campaign, followed by a narrowing of the Tory lead in the fourth week, and then a widening back again in the final few days of the campaign.

Table 5.3   General Election, 1979: who won the election
             itself?

	Change matrix (4–6 Apr to 4–6 May) electorate
	%
From Con	8.5
To Con	4.5
Net change	−4.0
From Lab	6.5
To Lab	6.5
Net change	0
Lab gain	+4

Source: MORI/*Sunday Times* panel

This pattern was followed among the panellists as well, and at
the end of the day the Labour party won the campaign (barely)
even though it lost the election. Because of the inaccuracy of
the Electoral Register at the date of the election, the effective
figure might be of the order of 83%.

That Labour won the campaign is shown in Table 5.3. Labour
won over 5% of Tories, and lost 3% in return, and in the
course of the campaign three-quarters of the 'don't knows'
made up their mind, and 33% went into the Labour camp
while 26% went to the Tories.

There is a stark lesson to be learned from the reasons
panellists gave for their election vote. Seven alternatives were
presented to each panel member who was asked to tell the
interviewer which of the reasons given were among those
determining their vote (only 6% said there were 'other reasons').
The top marks went to 'Believe the party I voted for will be
best at looking after the interests of people like me', selected by
58% overall, and 61% of both Conservative and Labour voters.

Otherwise, policies (62%) topped the Tories' choice, and habit (49%) led Labour voters' list.

More Labour voters than Tories (33% to 25%) gave 'Liked its leader(s)' as an important reason for their choice; more Tory voters than Labour (31% to 25%) gave 'Disliked the other party's policies' as an important reason for them. Only 16% indicated the local candidate played a role in their decision. Prices (55%) were only marginally ahead of strikes and industrial relations (52%) among the issues our panellists gave as important in helping them to decide for whom to vote, and law and order was also a key issue for Tory voters (58%), as was taxation (53%). Among Labour voters other important issues were unemployment (41%) and the NHS (26%).

On issues, the Labour party seemed to be winning the campaign (having started behind) till a week before election day. In the final week, however, much of the ground they had gained was lost back to the Tories; only on the issue of jobs and unemployment did the Labour party end up having won more voters than it lost over the campaign. In fact, the Labour party lost a net 9% of the electorate during the final week of the campaign on both strikes and taxes, and 4% on prices and 3% on jobs. The figures suggest the Tories finished strongly.

A number of changes characterized the private polling, although MORI was serving in its fourth General Election and ORC in its fifth. The change of Labour leadership meant Mr Callaghan was no longer party Treasurer, and his replacement, Norman Atkinson, was implacably opposed to polls. This, and the general increase in strength of the left wing, always cynical about the value of polls which inevitably showed the public less than enthusiastic about the Left's policy proposals, meant a tough fight for money for private polls, especially in the light of the extreme financial straits of the party. Moreover, MORI was now publishing other polls in the press, and was no longer the 'exclusive property' of Transport House. While this should not have mattered, it did.

These and other factors led to a relative reduction in budget for MORI's election polling, e.g. cutting the number of daily polls from 17 in the October 1974 23-day election period to ten in the longer (36-day) 1979 campaign. There were no Scottish election polls for the party — which was doing well there anyway — and no extra analysis budget. When Mr Wilson resigned, MORI lost a keen student of its work.

On the Tory side, the move of Humphrey Taylor to the United States meant a new face at the table and while his replacement, John Hanvey (awarded the CBE in the 1990 New Year's Honours list for 'political service'), was well enough regarded as a technician, he had less of the political and personal flair of his predecessor. He too had a less enthusiastic client in Mrs Thatcher than Taylor had had in Mr Heath.

According to the Labour Party Treasurer Norman Atkinson, the Labour party spent £87,000 on polls in 1978 and 1979, and Butler and Kavanagh estimate the Conservatives spent more with ORC during the election period itself than Labour did with MORI. ORC's work included four major 'State of Battle' surveys, six mid-week 'quickies', 11 post-tests and party election broadcasts, special surveys of Liberal–Tory marginals and three sets of Scottish surveys. Also, the Tories retained Saatchi & Saatchi as their advertising agency for the 1979 election, and Saatchi conducted its own qualitative research to assist in the development of its advertising effort.

A former politics lecturer and Nuffield Fellow and by then Labour MP, Austin Mitchell,[2] had this view of the 1979 election:

> More modern parties see the need for objective information of the type forthcoming from surveys of opinion. In 1978 such surveys provided early warnings of the changing predilections of the skilled worker, of the growing feeling for a 1978 election, of Labour's weak points. They can also provide much information about specific groups, and reactions to policies, individual issues and even the party generally. Yet polling needs to be done regularly to warn of trends and to allow the party to develop the skills and the habits of dealing with the information. This does not mean adopting the Tory approach of formulating policies just because they are popular, though in a democracy popularity has to be a major argument in favour of a policy and certainly not one against it. Rather the information is used as a chart of the territory through which the party has to trek. Polls bring knowledge of which subjects to tackle head on, which to strike,

which issues to push home and which to avoid, which policies will sell and which won't. Labour is as much in the merchandising business as the makers [of] biological Ariel. There is little point in confusing bad merchandising with high principle.

Weighting of the polling data

Adjustments for turnout had been employed to effect, by ORC, in the 1970 election. All random samples are weighted to contend with differential response. Sometimes, quota samples are as well. (See Part III for discussion of sampling methodology.) In 1979, several polling firms[3] used computer weighting techniques of one sort or another (Table 5.4).

Marplan[4] weighted in two stages, first interlocking sex, region and class and then 'the data was re-examined and there was found to be more people in the sample who claimed to vote Conservative in the last election than who claimed to vote Labour. To enable comparison with the earlier polls the data was then weighted to the profile of the claimed past voting

Table 5.4 Weighting effect, 1979

	Gallup			Marplan		
	Unwtd %	Wtd %	Diff. %	Unwtd %	Wtd %	Diff. %
Con	40.3	40.8	+0.5	41.0	38.9	−2.1
Lab	38.9	38.8	−0.1	31.4	33.5	+2.1
Lib	12.0	12.9	−0.9	13.2	11.8	−1.4
Nationalist	2.9	1.4	−1.5	2.3	2.6	+0.3
Other	1.1	1.1	0			
Would not vote				3.4	3.4	0
Refused/d.k.	5.1	5.2	+0.1	8.6	9.8	+1.2
Con lead	1.4	2.0	+0.6	9.6	5.4	−4.2

behaviour reported in their first two surveys.' Marplan's weighting factors were as large as 1.2 and 0.7.

Gallup[5] weighted by region by marginality of constituency at the last General Election. NOP[6] found 'the proportion working full time and the percentage of Trade Unionists were both about 3% short of expected figures. The differences between the voting intention of Unionist and non-Unionist observed in the previous poll (carried out 48 hours earlier) were used to calculate weights which were applied to the survey. This resulted in a reduction of the Conservative lead by about 3%.' NOP did not keep a precise record of their weighting. None of the newspaper reports of these polls explained the effect of the weighting nor even that weighting had been used.

RSL[7] employed a weighting procedure in their first election poll in 1979, which reduced the Conservative lead to 21%. The raw data produced a 22.5% Tory lead. The procedure used on this occasion was based on 'the assumption that the Liberal and other voters at the 1974 election would have been drawn in the ratio of 3.3 : 1 from people now claiming to have voted Conservative and Labour. Consequently to restore our results to this assumed distribution, we weighted claimed Conservative voters in 1974 × 0.952, and claimed Labour voters ×1.054. The 3.3 : 1 ratio was based on the finding that Liberal and other claimed voters in 1974 divided in these proportions in their 1979 voting intention.' RSL did not weight their subsequent three election surveys. Their weighting procedure was not described in the *Observer* articles.

Notes

1   David Butler and Dennis Kavanagh, *The British General Election of 1979* (Macmillan, 1980).

2   Austin Mitchell, *Can Labour Win Again?* (Fabian Society Tract, date), p. 19.

3   MORI's final (*Evening Standard*) poll was unweighted; its final *Daily Express* poll was a recall on electors interviewed ten days previously and those who responded to the call back were weighted

back to the earlier sample's voting intention figures to allow for differential response.

4   John Clemens, Letter to the author, 27 November 1979.
5   Robert Wybrow, Letter to the author, 5 November 1979.
6   John Barter, Letter to the author, 13 November 1979.
7   J. Cornish, Letter to the author, 31 October 1979.

6 The Rise and Fall of the SDP and the 'Falklands Factor'

Labour under Mr Callaghan actually led the Tories in 1980, but then came the Wembley Conference, the Healey–Benn Deputy Leadership contest, the Limehouse Declaration and the split-off of the 'Gang of Four' to found first the Council for Social Democracy which then evolved into the Social Democratic Party (SDP).

The Alliance of Liberals and the SDP soared to peak at 44% in the autumn of 1981 as Labour and the Tories sunk to 27% each. The scepticism of the critics (mainly supporters of the Conservative and Labour parties) of Britain's new political party turned increasingly to apprehension, and in some cases fear, as the party turned the well-publicized support reflected in the opinion polls into electoral success.

In July 1981, Roy Jenkins, the senior member of the 'Gang of Four' who led the new party, managed to turn a 9% Liberal share of the Warrington vote at the 1979 General Election into a 42% share at the Warrington by-election, standing as the candidate for the SDP with Liberal support. The Labour candidate, Doug Hoyle, standing in place of Sir Thomas Williams (whose appointment as a circuit judge precipitated the election), saw a 10,274 Labour majority slashed to 1,759 in what was previously considered one of the safer seats in the country.

In the Croydon North-West by-election in October 1981,

Liberal three-time loser William Pitt succeeded in winning a 3,254 majority for the Liberal party in alliance with the Social Democrats, in a seat previously held by the Conservatives with a 3,769 majority over Labour. It was a particularly notable win for a candidate who had failed to gain the one-eighth of the votes cast necessary to save his deposit in May 1979. And in late November of that year, Crosby, a 'safe' Tory seat with a majority of 19,000 at the General Election, fell to the SDP's Mrs Shirley Williams, again in alliance with the Liberal party. Thus in three quite different psephological tests, the new Alliance performed remarkably well and remarkably consistently. Clearly rumblings in the electorate were felt even above the foundations of No. 10 Downing Street and heard above the din created by the fight in the Labour party.

Following the launch of the SDP in March 1981, the national opinion polls showed a gradually increasing level of support strengthened by the alliance with the Liberal party.[1] The Liberals traditionally commanded a far higher level of support from the British electorate than their 11 out of 635 seats in the House of Commons suggested. In the February 1974 General Election the Liberals did exceptionally well to win 19% of the vote, yet this only gave them 14 seats. In May 1979, with 11% of the popular vote, they won just 11 parliamentary seats.

With the Social Democrats' determination to 'break the mould of British politics', both the Liberals and the SDP had a mutual interest in instigating a constitutional change to introduce proportional representation in British elections. In addition to that overriding ambition, both parties' commitment to remaining members of the European Community, their support for NATO and similar analyses of the ills of the British economy made them natural bedfellows. With each party determined to retain its separate identity, the extent of agreement between them was startling despite the obvious newsworthiness of perceptible cracks in their alliance. The SDP, and the Alliance, had an extraordinarily good press, and led many a critic to label the party as a media creation.

To some extent these critics were right. From the start, the SDP called on the services of professional public relations advisers to ensure the success of their launch; this obviously penetrated to how they treated the media.

In a country battered by economic recession, many people responded to the optimistic and confident tones of the Social Democrats as the best hope for recovery. The argument that the two party system reduced British politics to a battle between two entrenched ideologies with nothing new to offer Britain, was one many Britons, anxious for a scapegoat, (or clutching at straws?) found easy to embrace.

The party clearly attracted many previously politically inactive people to swell its ranks as well as former supporters of the two old parties. A survey of 376 delegates to the London conference of the SDP in October that year showed that 58% of delegates had never been a member of a political party other than the SDP before and 85% had never stood as a candidate for a political party in either a local or national election. Many, probably most, of the 51,800-odd members recruited in the first eight weeks after the party's launch must also have been previously inactive politically. Its membership stood at about 70,000 at the end of its first year.

To say that the Social Democrats were a media creation was, however, something of a trivialization of its by-election and indeed local election achievements. The new party took every opportunity to use the media to its best advantage and the newsworthiness of the party meant the media and the SDP had a mutual interest in reaching even larger audiences. But this could not have happened if the new party had not already been well equipped for the launch. The 'Gang of Four' had all previously been Cabinet ministers in Labour governments of the 1960s and 1970s. Besides having had experience of government at a very senior level, three, at least, were also well known and well regarded among the British electorate. Their ministerial experience enhanced both their credibility and the credibility of the new party they had set out to establish.

However, the success of the new party and the alliance with the Liberals probably owed more to the decline in support for the two parties which dominated British politics for over half a century than to any other factor. Two and a half years into their administration, polls showed the Conservative government to have lost nearly half the support it had at the time of the 1979 General Election; satisfaction with the performance of the government was almost at its lowest point since its election; and satisfaction with the way Mrs Thatcher was doing her job as Prime Minister was little better. The decline in her own and the government's popularity was gradual, but largely consistent, since the spring of 1980.

Neither did the official Opposition present itself much more favourably to the British public. Satisfaction with Michael Foot as Leader of the Opposition was then even lower than with Mrs Thatcher, and his popularity showed a similar decline from the autumn of the previous year, when he took over from Mr Callaghan. Liberal party leader David Steel was the only one of the three main party leaders for whom more electors expressed satisfaction than dissatisfaction – indeed, in October by a substantial net +20%.

The Labour party's internal battles regarding the deputy leadership, and concern with its constitution rather than with the main issues facing the country, probably had much to do with the party's poor showing in the opinion polls. At the same time many people who turned from Labour in May 1979 and voted Conservative were probably reluctant to switch back again if they could find no strong reason for returning to the Labour fold.

The rise of the SDP/Liberal Alliance, then, owed much to the poor image of the other two main parties in Britain, and of their leaders. In one important respect, however, the Alliance's popularity was enigmatic. Normally one would expect a party, or alliance, which is ahead in the polls, and capable of winning by-elections, to be seen also as the party with the best policies, especially on the issues of most concern to the electorate. The evidence in the polls at that time was that this was not the case.

A MORI poll in Croydon the week before the October by-election showed that only 6% of the electorate believed the SDP had the best policies on unemployment, 8% thought the Liberals did, 14% the Conservatives and 41% Labour, yet this was the issue considered by a huge majority to be the most important facing Britain. Inflation, the second most important issue, found 27% who felt Labour had the best policies, 25% the Conservatives, yet only 7% the Liberals and 6% the SDP. The poor standing of both the Liberals and SDP was similar for all the other issues considered, ranging from the Common Market to education and public transport. At Crosby, the week before that by-election, a MORI poll showed that electors felt the Conservatives had better policies than the SDP on the major issues — yet the SDP won.

Although the SDP was founded on a commitment to certain policy stances — particularly continued membership of the Common Market, support for NATO, and proportional representation — it was found that many of its supporters were opposed to these positions. The SDP's commitment to consultation with its membership on policy (and constitutional issues, such as how to elect its leaders) meant the electorate had to wait until well into the following year before finding out in detail the policies on which it was to stand. The party's leaders issued some statements on the kind of policies — particularly in the economic field — they thought the party would support.

The close alliance with the Liberal party, whose policies had been developed over many years of opposition, did give the electorate some indication of the sort of policies the new party was likely to support. None the less, it was difficult not to conclude that support for the SDP was based more upon despair with the failure of Labour or Conservative policies to deal with Britain's problems than on any detailed appreciation of policies the new party was likely to pursue.

The Conservative party had traditionally been the party of the middle classes — the managers, teachers, professional and white-collar workers — while Labour appealed most to the working classes — the blue-collar skilled, semi-skilled and unskilled workers. With the middle classes then comprising only a third of the electorate, the Conservatives had to rely on winning a substantial proportion of the working class vote to ensure their return to office.

Detailed analysis of opinion polls from the time of the two previous General Elections, in October 1974 and May 1979, showed the extent of the electoral damage done to the Conservative and Labour parties. It was the massive swing of both the skilled and semi-/unskilled working classes to the Conservatives between the two elections which gave the Tories a comfortable 44-seat clear majority in the House of Commons in 1979.

Whereas in October 1974 the Conservatives had only 26% of the skilled-working-class vote and 22% of the semi-/unskilled vote, by May 1979 these figures had risen to 41% and 34% respectively, with both the Labour and Liberal parties suffering significant declines. Paradoxically, Labour's loss of 8% of the working-class vote contrasted with an increase of 5% in its share of the middle-class vote. The Conservative gains were particularly marked among the new voters. Their share of the 18–24-year-old vote in 1979 had increased by 18% (from 24% to 42%) between the two elections, mainly at the expense of the Liberals.

The decline in Conservative support after their victory in May 1979 was not just the result of a swing of these groups away from them. There was a desertion of some 17% of the working classes and 22% of the 18–24 age group, including four out of every five semi- and unskilled working-class respondents in this age group. But they also lost a substantial amount of support among the middle classes – decline of 14% – and all other age groups ranging from 11% of those 55 and over, 18% of 25–34-year-olds, and 19% of 35–54-year-olds. The rise in Alliance support meant that the Labour party failed to regain its 1974 (40%) share of the vote and its 1981 level of 38% represented no net overall improvement since the May 1979 General Election.

The detailed analysis, however, showed this 'no change' presentation to be a misleading one. Labour had, for example, more than won back the support it had lost in some groups, gained support in others and lost ground to the new Alliance in still others. With a 48% share they were particularly successful in winning back the young (18–24) (especially working-class) vote. Their middle-class gain in the 1979 election was almost wiped out but compensated for by a 3–4% gain in the somewhat larger working-class vote. While Labour's 3% gain among the middle-aged (35–54) reflects only a working-class swing, the decline in support among older voters (over 55) applied to middle- and working-class respondents, men and women.

These findings clearly indicated that the SDP had not arisen merely as a result of straight switching of votes from an unpopular government, but succeeded in drawing substantial nearly equal support from both the major parties.

Although past voting recall is known not to be a totally reliable measure of actual voting in previous elections, it does give a broad indication which can be used to analyse the sources of current party support. A MORI poll in September 1981 showed that 10% of those who said they voted Labour in 1979 said then they would vote Social Democrat, and 3% said they would vote Liberal, compared with 1% who had switched allegiance to the Conservatives.

The MORI survey among electors in Warrington just after the by-election showed that an astounding 60% of those who said they had previously voted Conservative had switched their allegiance to the SDP; this resulted in the Conservative losing his deposit, winning only 7% of the vote. Of those who said they had voted Labour in 1979, just under a third (29%) switched to the SDP – an almost equal loss in terms of number of votes.

A poll conducted by MORI in the two days preceding the Liberal/SDP Alliance victory in the Croydon North-West constituency showed votes coming equally from Labour and Conservative. Nearly a third of those who said they had voted Conservative (31%) and Labour (32%) in 1979 had switched their allegiance to the Alliance candidate.

The by-election in 'safe' Conservative-held Crosby also showed substantial desertions from those claiming to have voted either Conservative or Labour in 1979. The Alliance won 35% of Conservative support and 62% of Labour support, a mirror image of the 'safe' Labour seat of Warrington.

The shift of support to the Social Democrats was interpreted by some observers as yet more evidence of the breakdown of class as a major determinant of British political allegiance. Not only had the working class vote, in particular, become more volatile but the willingness of electors to identify with a particular social class had declined markedly over the last two decades. A MORI poll in May 1981 showed only 29% saying they thought of themselves as belonging to a particular social class, compared with 50% who did in 1964.[2] Furthermore, only 15% of the total thought of themselves as working class, fewer than half of the proportion in 1964. For Labour, this was bad news. At one time simply being 'working class' was a sufficiently good reason to vote Labour.

With the government's monetarist policies increasingly criticized by its own ministers and backbenchers as well as the press, and the Labour party preoccupied with its internal struggles, the Alliance was given a clear run and plenty of opportunity to woo the electorate. Up to then the media was sympathetic, but this changed over time.

The Alliance peaked at 44% in November 1981 as Labour and the Tories sunk to 27% each. This was triple the 14% share of the vote the Liberals received in the 1979 General Election. The Alliance lost half of their gain in the early months of 1982 as squabbles over party leadership, candidate selection and determination of policy stances took their toll. A MORI poll published in the third week of March showed that the Alliance share had fallen to 30%, and on 2 April 1982 the troops of President Galtieri of Argentina invaded the Falkland Islands.

The 'Falklands Factor'

From the first news of the landing of Argentinian forces on the Falkland Islands on 2 April, MORI polled the British public's reaction to the situation almost every week. Ten polls were taken: a panel study of four waves for *The Economist* (and one wave for BBC's *Panorama*), two separate polls for the *Sunday Times*, two more for *Panorama* and one for the *Daily Star*. These followed a 'base-line' survey which was in the field at the time of the initial landing.[3]

At the start of April, the parties were just about even with the Tories at 33%. By the time the Falklands War ended on 18 June, the Tory share had soared to 52%. Opinion polls were not the only measure of the political mood of the country. Just one month after the news of the Falklands invasion hit the headlines of British newspapers, local government elections took place in Britain. These elections, largely a referendum on the performance of the government of the day, customarily swing heavily against the party in power. On that occasion, however, extrapolation of local government results to the national picture showed the Conservatives at 40%, Labour 31% and the Alliance at 26%. Hundreds of seats that had been expected to go to the Alliance stayed Tory (especially in the South of England where the Alliance had been running second to the Conservatives) and to Labour (especially in the North which is more urban and more pro-Labour) stayed Tory. Two by-elections took place during the Falklands conflict. Both were expected to show Alliance strength. The Conservatives won both handily. The conclusion was unavoidable: the South Atlantic crisis was extremely good for the party in power.

The public mood towards the handling of the Falklands War — coming as it did totally out of the blue — was initially one of cautious, wait-and-see support for the government. The conflict started badly for the Cabinet with the resignation of Foreign Secretary Carrington and two of his deputies. As the crisis developed, however, the level of satisfaction with the way the government handled the situation improved steadily — from 60% approval in early April to 84% in late May.

It is often easier to know what opinion poll questions should have been asked after the fact than to know which questions should be asked at the time the questionnaire is developed. The base-line questionnaire for the panel was developed while British ships were steaming towards the Falklands, before the precise nature of the conflict was clear.

To cover any eventuality, a series of should/should not questions, was devised on 'whether Britain should take/have taken the following measures over the Falkland Islands situation'. These ranged from measures taken immediately, such as severing diplomatic relations with Argentina (71% agreed), banning Argentinian imports into Britain (84%) and freezing Argentinian assets in British banks (82%), to measures supported by roughly one in four of the British public who were hawkish to the point of wishing to intern Argentinian citizens residing in Great Britain (24%), to bomb Argentinian military and naval bases on the mainland (28%) and land troops on the Argentinian mainland (21%). An incredible one in 20 believed the situation called for the use of nuclear weapons against Argentina (or, as one lady put it 'if we have to "nuke" Rio (sic) to regain the Falklands, then we'll do it!').

Initially there was some doubt in the British public's mind about the importance of retaining British sovereignty over the Falklands if it resulted in the loss of British servicemen's lives (44% believed it important enough, 49% disagreed). There was even less enthusiasm if carrying the war to the Falklands caused the loss of Falkland Islanders' lives (36% yes, 55% no).

As the crisis developed and the island of South Georgia was taken without loss of life, the answers to the conditional question turned from negative to positive, with 51% in agreement that the loss of servicemen's lives could be justified in the 20–21 April survey to 58% in the 23–24 April survey, then down slightly to 53% early in May after the first loss of life, and finally to 62% at the end of May.

This slight hesitation occurred at the time of the sinking on 2 May of the Argentinian warship *General Belgrano* by a British submarine with a reported 1,000-plus men on board. On 4 May, *HMS Sheffield* was sunk by an Argentinian Exocet missile and 20 British sailors lost their lives. Fieldwork was going on between 3 and 5 May. An examination of the findings showed that the downturn in confidence was occasioned by the sudden loss of life, i.e., with the sinking of the *General Belgrano*, rather than the loss of British lives specifically. With the death toll rising into the hundreds, the late May findings showed that although nearly two-thirds of those questioned believed retaining sovereignty was justification enough for the loss of lives, 34% disagreed. This issue of 'proportionality' remained the hardest for polling questions to elucidate.

The most constant figure of all was concern about the issue

of sovereignty. At the outset, just half (51%) of the British public said they 'care very much' whether Britain regains sovereignty over the Falkland Islands. The 'care very much' figure remained at about that level.

Throughout the conflict there were a number of proposals put forward for the solution of the Falkland Islands crisis. At the outset, one option — that the Falklands should become Argentinian territory but be leased back to the British government for administration — was favoured by 26% and opposed by 63%. In May, the figures had hardly shifted — 23% in favour and 64% opposed. Other proposals included a joint Argentinian/British civil administration with the United States as overseer and islanders involved. More people opposed than favoured this proposal as well (49% to 39%). However, a majority (57%) in the early May panel felt it wrong 'to go to war then if the government was willing to give up the Falkland Islands in the long term'.

In a separate 16 May survey for the BBC current affairs flagship *Panorama*, the public felt that in any negotiation with Argentina over the Falkland Islands the withdrawal of Argentinian troops should be insisted upon by the British government (90%); the Argentinian flag should be removed from the Falklands during negotiation (69%); full British administration of the islands should be restored immediately (70%); Argentina should recognize British sovereignty of the Falklands pending a final agreement (75%); and the Falkland Islanders should have the final say in any settlement (62%). But, a narrow plurality felt that 'it is not essential for Argentina to recognize full British sovereignty forever', and a majority believed that it was acceptable to transfer sovereignty to a United Nations trusteeship (51% to 43%).

By mid-May, the patience of the British War Cabinet with the drawn-out negotiations process had worn thin — and that of the public with it. Continued British attacks on the Port Stanley airfield, the failure of the Haig peace initiative, of the Peruvian plan and of the United Nations negotiations, all led to a widespread acceptance of the inevitability of escalation of the conflict. When asked, 'If negotiations do break down, which of the following options on this card would you favour?' 59% of the sample were by then for a full-scale invasion of the Falklands, and 34% even felt Britain should bomb military bases in Argentina.

During the time of the landing and as British losses mounted, some observers expected public support to begin to dwindle. In fact, the opposite occurred. By that time the *Sheffield* had been lost, Sea King helicopters had been ditched, Harriers had been shot down, *HMS Antelope* was sinking and scores of lives had been lost, but 80% of those polled thought on 23 May that the government was right to go ahead with the landing on the Falklands.

By that time, a majority (54%) felt that Britain should retain the Falklands forever; there was also a majority, however, in favour of handing the islands over to a UN trusteeship (51% favourable, 43% against by 25–26 May). This overlap probably reflected a deep-seated conviction that victory was essential to restore British status and pride – yet a subsequent compromise was inevitable.

The picture of the Falklands conflict conveyed by the polls organizations was perhaps predictable from previous instances of democracies engaged in 'just wars'. As in the early stages of Suez and Vietnam (and this is not an attempt to draw either a political or a military parallel), domestic support for both the action and the government prosecuting it tended to be high. In the case of Suez, it should be said, although opinion was eventually equivocal on the merit of the expedition, support for the Eden government and even for Eden himself remained high throughout. Although he subsequently resigned (due to quite genuine ill-health) his Conservative party went on to win a resounding election victory two years later. Mrs Thatcher's administration did the same a year after the Falklands War.[4]

Notes

1   Robert M. Worcester and Peter F. Hutton, 'The British Political' Scene', *Public Opinion Magazine*, November 1981.

2   David Butler and Donald Stokes, *Political Change in Britain*, 2nd end (Macmillan, 1969).

3   Robert M. Worcester and Simon Jenkins, 'Britain Rallies 'Round the Prime Minister', *Public Opinion Magazine*, July 1982.

4   For an excellent psephological analysis of the 'Falkland Factor' see Helmut Norpoth, 'The Falklands War and Government Popularity in Britain: Rally without Consequence or Surge without Decline?', *Electoral Studies*, 1987, 3–16. 6, no. 1, pp.

7 The 1983 Thatcher Triumph

The Tories entered 1983 with 44% support to Labour's 35% and the Alliance at 20%. Through the first four months the Tories floated around the 42–45% level, Labour 30–35% and the Alliance in the low 20s. Two by-elections enlivened the spring of 1983. At Bermondsey in late February, in a Catholic, working-class, dockyard constituency, a left-wing constituency Labour party put up a personally and politically unacceptable candidate whom the voters firmly rejected in favour of the Liberal. This caused a surge of Alliance support nationally at the expense of the Labour party that proved short-lived when a month later a more appropriate Labour candidate overcame an early poll deficit to defeat an ineffective SDP/Alliance challenger at Darlington.[1]

Perhaps of greater moment was a steady rise in the public's view of the recovery in the economy. In the third week of January just 22% of the public said they expected the general economic condition of the country to improve over the next 12 months. By February the figure was 26%, in March 31% and by 17–23 April it was 36%. Calling the election on 9 May caught the flood tide.

The progress of the 1983 campaign

The first poll of the 1983 campaign was a MORI phone-out, face-to-face interview, phone-back results, without the sending back of questionnaires for analysis. MORI's aggregate analysis of 13,926 respondents excluded this survey, as did the breakdown of our polls in the four weeks of the campaign. Thus our 'Progress of the Campaign' analysis began with the Alliance at their low point of the campaign, 15%, and ended with them up at 26%, an 11% rise. During the period the Alliance rose slowly at first among all groups, accelerating at the end of the campaign. Their rise was fairly uniform, least among people living in the Midlands (up 8% from 15% to 23%) and greatest among the middle class (ABC1s) (up 13% from 15% to 28%). There was no difference in the Alliance share from the beginning of the campaign to the end whichever party's candidate, SDP or Liberal, was standing.

There was more shifting among the other major parties. Overall, the Tories lost 3% (47% to 44%), but among younger people, the 18–34 age group, the Tories began and finished at the same level, having risen four points during the first two weeks and gone back down at the end. The Labour party lost the 1983 campaign as no party has ever lost a campaign before, dropping eight points, from 36% to 28%, a quarter of its support, over the four-week period. Labour's losses were greatest among younger people (−12%), council house tenants (−11%) and among C2s (−10%).

Polls in Britain ask a two-part voting intention question, first asking people how they intend to vote, when usually between 20% and 25% of the British say they are 'undecided', 5–6% say they 'will not vote' and usually only 2% refuse to say how they intend to vote. Those who are 'undecided' or 'refuse' are then asked which party they are 'most inclined' to support or 'lean toward'. This second question tests not only the firmness of the electorate generally ('don't knows' usually rise in the early stages of a campaign and then drop towards the end) but also the relative firmness of support for each party. In the 1983 election the firmness for each of the parties was nearly equal, with the Labour vote, if anything, slightly firmer although of course from a smaller, bed-rock, base.

In addition to the two-part voting intention question, MORI

takes three other strength-of-feeling measures: 'certainty of voting', 'care about the outcome', and 'mind made up' or 'may change mind'. These 'strength' measures indicated how relatively weakly the young regarded the election, how the (resigned?) working class did not care as strongly as did middle-class people about the outcome, and how relatively uncertain Alliance supporters were in mid campaign about their support.

One always interesting analysis is the matrix of current voting intention by previous voting recall. Of course, memories are faulty and frequently half the people who voted Liberal at the last election forget they did so. On 2 June, a week before polling day, of recalled 1979 Tory voters, 83% remained loyal, while among 1979 Labour supporters, only 64% were staying Labour, more than three times as many moving to the Alliance (26%) than to the Conservatives (7%). Three-quarters of Liberals in 1979 said they would stick with the Alliance candidate; of Liberal defectors, three times as many intended to shift to Mrs Thatcher (19%) as to Labour (6%).

Our recall survey of respondents first interviewed on 26 and 31 May and then re-interviewed on 6–7 June showed clearly how little switching there was between the two major parties. The main erosion was from Labour, only 84% of whose end-of-May support stayed loyal; 13% of Labour's supporters went to the Alliance and only 1% to the Conservatives in the final week of the campaign.

The issues of the campaign

Although from the beginning to the end of the campaign unemployment was expressed as the most important issue, the two issues of the campaign where the argument was joined were defence and disarmament, and the management of the economy/cost of living/etc. The interventions by former Labour Prime Minister James Callaghan and Labour Deputy Leader Denis Healey drew attention to the defence/disarmament issues.

From before the campaign began it was clear that the Labour

party, while ahead on the unemployment issue, was not thought to have policies to reduce it that could be afforded. That unemployment was the problem was widely agreed; that Labour had affordable solutions was widely disputed, even by Labour's own supporters. Only about a third (36%) of the electorate thought Labour could succeed in reducing unemployment, and although this was twice as many as thought the Conservatives would cause the level of unemployment to fall (18%), the average expectation was that under a Labour government Britain would have about three million unemployed in two years' time and about four million if the Tories were returned.

During the course of the campaign, and immediately before, the Conservatives won the debate on defence, on 'one-sided' disarmament as they described it, and on the use of Cruise as a negotiating ploy and even Trident as the replacement of Polaris. Labour had the initiative six months prior to the election, with widespread public support for banning Cruise and cancelling Trident. By going too far, calling for abandoning Polaris and for unilateral nuclear disarmament they drove away the breadth of their support. Labour Leader Michael Foot's insistence on returning again and again during the campaign to his long-time theme of unilateral nuclear disarmament may have been popular with his audiences of hundreds of Labour supporters, but it turned off the millions watching him on television.

Another campaign theme thought by Labour to have public support was the call to leave the Common Market. It was never shown by Labour how this could effectively be done, and if Britain stayed in, Mrs Thatcher was the leader whom the public thought would get the best deal for Britain, which was really what most electors wanted. Thus once again competence was the issue behind the issue.

The public did believe Labour's policies were to be preferred on the 'caring society' issues of the National Health Service, social services and pensions. An effective ploy was the £58 weekly pension rise, as was Labour's attempts to focus the campaign on these issues. But just when they would schedule their press conference on one or another of these themes, one or another of their 'own goals' would divert public attention.

Political leadership

Mr Foot began the campaign with the lowest satisfaction score any party leader had ever suffered. He was seen as incapable of controlling his party and incompetent as a potential Prime Minister. While widely respected as a nice person and regarded with affection by many Labour supporters, the young especially, few regarded him as a match for Mrs Thatcher on any of the qualities regarded as important.

Liberal leader David Steel (+26%), even more than Mrs Thatcher (+9%), was regarded as having the best campaign. Dr David Owen, the new SDP leader (+7%), and Neil Kinnock, the likely new Labour leader (+6%), Dennis Healey (+5%) and Shirley Williams (SDP) (+5%), were 'up' at mid campaign (before Healey's 'slaughter' remark and Kinnock's 'guts' comment). SDP leader Roy Jenkins (−5%) and Michael Foot (−29%) were bottom of the poll.

Party image

Only the Alliance rose in the esteem of the British public during the campaign (+9%); the Tories lost ground (−15%) and Labour plummeted (−38%). The Conservatives loss was greatest among men (−22%), middle-aged people (35−54) (−22%) and DEs (the unskilled and those on state pension) (24%). Labour's image fell uniformly among men (−39%) and women (−39%), less with 18−24-year-olds (−23%) and with DEs (−28%); the Alliance did better with women (+11%) and with 25−34-year-olds (+18%).

The final polls

In 1983 most of the polls overestimated the Tories' share, most underestimated Labour's, all, save Audience Selection, were exactly correct for the Alliance share (Table 7.1). Audience Selection, polling by telephone, was the first to conduct a national telephone poll as an eve-of-poll prediction and their wide margin of error threw a shadow on the use of such polls in the period that followed.

What happened?

There was a structural shift in the electorate which in nearly every case benefited the Conservative. Middle-class voters, non-trade unionists, people living in the South of England and, especially owner-occupiers were not only more likely to vote Tory than when Mrs Thatcher first took up office; their numbers had increased. Further, there were massive shifts of public support away from the Labour party to the Alliance, and in fact, even the Conservatives actually lost share from the 45% level they had in May 1979 to 44%. The 'breaking of the mould of British politics' did indeed occur, but not in the way the SDP hoped. Between 1979 and 1983 the Alliance added 12% to the Liberal 1979 base of 14%. Ten per cent of these votes came from Labour and 1% each from the Tories and from 'others', mainly the Scottish Nationalist Party.

From the launch of the SDP, the Alliance had more support from women than men, from middle-aged people rather than younger or elderly people, from and middle-class rather than working-class people. Yet the evenness of their support across the regions also tended to be mirrored in demographic analysis. Startlingly, the group among which Alliance support was strongest was middle-class/women/trade unionists – the women members of NALGO (local government officers), USDAW (shop workers), BIFU (bank workers), ASTMS (scientific technicians), etc. Among middle-class (white-collar) trade unionists, then up to 40% of the British trade union movement, the Alliance was in second place after the Tories, pushing Labour, the 'party of the trade unions', into third place.

In Britain, the 'Gender Gap' traditionally favours the Conservative party. Women are usually more likely, by some 5–10% to support the Tories than Labour, about half caused

Table 7.1 General Election, 1983

Poll	Aud. Sel.*	Harris	Gallup	Marplan	NOP	MORI	Actual result
Newspaper	Sun	Daily Express	Daily Telegraph	Guardian	Daily Mail	London Standard	
Fieldwork	7 Jun	7–8 Jun	7–8 Jun	8 Jun	6–7 Jun	8 Jun	9 Jun
Sample size	(1,100)	(567R)	(2,003)	(1,335)	(1,040)	(1,101)	
	%	%	%	%	%	%	%
Con	46	47	45.5	46	46	44	44
Lab	23	25	26.5	26	28	28	28
All	29	26	26	26	24	26	26
Other	2	2	2	2	2	2	2
Con lead	+23	+22	+19	+20	+18	+16	+16
Error on lead	+7	+6	+3	+4	+2	0	(4.3)
Average error on share (+/−)	2.2	1.5	0.8	1.0	1.0	0.0	(1.1)
Maximum error	5	3	1.5	2	2	0	(2.3)

* Telephone

by women's longevity and the propensity of older people to vote Tory. Even in October 1974, when Labour last had achieved a majority, more women voted Conservative than Labour. For the four elections prior to 1983 women were a steady 2% more Liberal (or SDP) than men.

In 1979, the C2s (the skilled working class) were 'the battle-ground of the election' and swung more than twice as much to the Tories than did the electorate as a whole in that election. In 1983 they swung back not at all; in fact, C2s swung equally to the others. While in 1974 Labour had a 23% lead over the Tories among C2s, in 1983 the Conservative led by 8%, a swing of 15% over the decade. Among C2 women, the Conservative lead was 14% and among older C2 women their lead was 19%. They had the support of nearly half (48%) of older C2 women (and 39% of their menfolk).

Notes

1   David Butler and Dennis Kavanagh, *The British General Election of 1983* (Macmillan, 1984).

8 Thatcher's Third Victory: 1987

1983–1987

Public support for each party remained static during the long hot summer of 1983 following the election. The status quo, Conservatives at 44% (+/−2%), Labour 28% (+/−2%) and the Alliance 26% (+/−2%), was repeated in poll after poll until the replacement of Michael Foot by Neil Kinnock as party Leader at the Labour Conference in October 1983. At a stroke, Labour's share jumped nine points, to 37%, three points coming from the Tories whose support fell to 41% and six from the Alliance, whose share went to 20%.

So it stayed until the start of the miners' strike in March 1984. Although the political journalists' collective wisdom is that the miners' strike damaged Labour, the figures do not bear this out. The 'Kinnock Factor' held up through the summer of 1984; in fact, Labour pulled even with the Tories that June, pulled three points ahead in July, and were back level-pegging in August. But in September 1984, after the TUC Conference, the Tories again took the lead and this widened to 8% following a disrupted Labour Conference and the bombing of the 1984 Conservative Party Conference hotel in Brighton, when the 'Thatcher Factor' took over once again.

At the midpoint of the second Thatcher term, the turn of the year 1985 saw the public's patience wearing thin on the miners' strike (a MORI poll for the *Sunday Times* showed 60%

of the public thought the government had handled the dispute poorly for the country as a whole and only 29% thought the government had handled it well). The public's patience was also wearing thin on economic and social issues.

Confidence in the Conservative government was shown to be waning. At the turn of the year:

- 70% of the British public expected the number of unemployed to rise in 1985 (only 6% did not);
- 59% expected the rate of inflation to rise (only 9% did not);
- 52% expected their own standard of living to fall (19% did not);
- 39% expected the number of strikes to rise (20% expected the number of strikes to fall).

A set of MORI's findings was presented by ITV's *Weekend World* team in a television special to mark the anniversary of the miners' strike. It showed a high degree of concern among the public over the state of the nation. The same poll showed a two-to-one support for altering the government's course on economic policy and for adopting measures directly to create jobs even at the risk of higher inflation. It also found 38% who said they faced the problem of not having enough money to make ends meet, 34% feared unemployment for their children, 25% feared unemployment for themselves, and of two-thirds of the country who believed Britain was more divided, an overwhelming 80% thought the government should introduce policies aimed more directly at reducing divisions in British society.

This then was the scene that faced the political parties beginning their preparations for the next General Election two-and-a-half or three years away. The Conservatives were firmly in office, if not in popular support; Labour was doing better in the polls than in getting their act together and the Alliance, although doing comparatively well in the polls, was under split leadership, was still squabbling over seats and policies, and was poorly financed.

The local elections in the shire countries in May 1985 (London and other metropolitan authorities and Scotland were not involved) were widely misinterpreted. They were a disaster for the Tories, good for the Alliance (especially the Liberals, who had picked the prime seats), and very good for Labour — showing that on those results in a General Election they would have formed the government. Labour's last election victory had come under Harold Wilson in October 1974, more than a decade before, when their 40 to 37% lead gave them a three-seat majority in the House of Commons (the Liberals were at 19%). From that election there was a 9% swing to the Conservatives across their two election victories, plus a bonus from redistricting. This meant, roughly, that a nine point swing to Labour from the 1983 General Election would be required for Neil Kinnock, to become Prime Minister.

The MORI poll for the *London Standard* in June 1985 showed Labour two points ahead: 35% to 33%, with the Alliance at 30%. At that level, a 2% swing to Labour at the expense of the Tories would have put the Labour party into power. That swing could come from the Alliance taking Tory support away, say to the 32% level for the Alliance, dropping the Tories to 31%, or through Labour attracting only two out of a hundred Tories who were disaffected by what they saw as ineffective Tory policies causing further social and economic divisions.

The Labour party was then seen by the public to have more of the better policies to solve the problems the country faced, especially on unemployment, but not, importantly, on solving the economic problems of the country. Further, a calculation by Dr Gordon Reece of Bristol University showed that while only a 23% share kept Labour in second place, it took 32% for the Tories and a staggering, and some said unfair, 40% for the Alliance to form a government. At 35% Labour could form a government.

The Conservatives were seen to have the best leadership, but their strength was thought a potential weakness if the long-awaited economic miracle did not arrive soon. 'Time for a change' was thought to be a powerful election slogan to a country which had given a government two full terms and was still awaiting a turndown in unemployment, promised tax cuts and economic prosperity.

The Alliance needed a hung Parliament. Having two leaders was to become more and more of a liability as the election approached, and yet there was no way that a single leader could be chosen. Alliance policies were still ill-understood, their front bench spokesmen were largely unknown, some of their former well-known leaders had faded and the electoral system was working against them.

Alliance supporters were without strong commitment; polls showed their supporters to be less committed to vote for them, many of their supporters preferred the policies of the other parties if not their leaders (in the EEC European Parliament election in 1984, 45% of people who voted for Alliance candidates favoured Britain getting out of the EEC despite the Alliance identification with strong European ties), and their supporters were nearly twice as likely to say they might switch to vote for another party than were the people who supported the two main parties.

Opinion polls generally have received the close attention of psephologists and political scientists in their election studies. Political opinion polling, especially voting intention, came under increased scrutiny in the run-up to the 1987 General Election, as from the turn of the year, or even a month or two before, the stock market, the strength of sterling and especially the gilt market were affected by the ups and downs of the fortunes of the Conservative party in the polls.

In the autumn of 1986 the Labour party and the Conservative party for several months were neck and neck. Round the turn of the year, one poll found a 5% Labour lead. This was at a time when commercial markets were quiet, there were no industrial disputes in the news, there was no significant government policy announced. The only news of the day was the switch in the polls to a significant lead for Labour. The effect of the publication of this poll and the rumours that preceded it were to clip 2 cents off the value of sterling against the American dollar. When the market closed in London the pound stood at $1.53. That evening the poll showing a Labour lead was published and the next morning the pound opened at $1.51. Yet the election was six months away at the earliest and in any case that poll was at variance with seven out of the eight polls published during the period.[1]

Over the months between the publication of that poll and the calling of the General Election, every shift and swing in an opinion poll caused the price of sterling to flutter, the stock market to rise and fall and, as was commented up on by a number of economic journalists and economists, the gilt market was driven almost entirely by the findings of each successive opinion poll.

The General Election of 1987

In 1987, all the major opinion polling companies did a creditable job, six out of six had the share of each party to within the plus or minus 3% margin of error generally accepted, as they all had done in 1983 (Audience Selection by telephone, excepted) and in 1979. During the month-long campaign, some 54 national opinion polls were reported, including straightforward national surveys and various polls conducted in collections of marginal constituencies.

In addition, there were at least seven Scottish polls, a poll in Wales, four national telephone polls, a dozen or so regional polls and several score individual constituencies polls published, plus at least 40-50 private polls conducted for the political parties and in some cases leaked to the press. There were two 'exit' polls, by Gallup for the BBC and by Harris for ITN which interviewed voters on the eve of (Gallup) and on the day of (both) the election. Gallup's result was less than satisfactory, underestimating the Conservative share by 3% and overestimating Labour's by 3%, resulting in a projected lead in seats of 26, 75 short of the actual result (see Table 8.2).

At the outset of the campaign the Conservatives enjoyed a lead of 42% over Labour's 32% and the Alliance's 24%. On election day, the Conservatives were up a point, Labour up two

Table 8.1   General Election, 1987

Poll	Aud. Sel.*	Harris	Gallup	Marplan	NOP	MORI	Actual result
Newspaper	Sun	TV-AM	Daily Telegraph	Guardian	Independent	The Times	
Fieldwork	9 Jun	10 Jun	8–9 Jun	10 Jun	10 Jun	9–10 Jun	11 Jun
Sample size:	1,702	2,122	2,005	1,633	1,668	1,688	
	%	%	%	%	%	%	%
Con	43	42	41	42	42	44	43
Lab	34	35	34	35	35	32	32
Alln	21	21	23.5	21	21	22	23
Other	2	2	1.5	2	2	2	2
Con lead	+9	+7	+7	+7	+7	+12	11
Error on lead	−2	−4	−4	−4	−4	+1	(3.2)
Average error on share (+/−)	1	1.5	1.25	1.5	1.5	0.5	(1.2)
Maximum error	2	3	2	3	3	1	(2.3)

*Telephone

Table 8.2   Exit polls, 1987

Poll	TV	Con	Lab	Alln	Lead	Seats
		%	%	%	%	
Harris	ITN	42	33	23	11	68
Gallup	BBC	40	35	23	5	26
Result		43	32	23	11	101

and the Alliance down three. The MORI/*Sunday Times* panel survey showed it was not as clear as that, as between the time the election was called and the weekend before polling day some 7.5 million people out of an electorate of some 43 million had changed their minds either between parties or on whether or not to vote. During the campaign itself, despite frequent comments by politicians and pundits to the contrary, the polls were remarkably stable. A week or so before polling day 21 out of the last 21 polls published had showed the Conservatives at 43% plus or minus 3%, Labour at 34% plus or minus 3% and the Alliance at 22% plus or minus 3%.

The 'Thatcher Revolution'

Wherein lay the support that made possible the hat-trick of Tory victories? In the following section trends in the key sub-groups of the electorate are broken down to show where the Labour party's efforts to persuade its potential supporters succeeded and failed; and where the decline in Alliance support took place.

Figures 8.1 (p. 104) and 8.2 (p. 106) show statistics for the more important geographic and demographic subgroupings, indicating changes in voting behaviour between 1983 and 1987. The figures were compiled by MORI and published in the *Sunday Times* immediately following the June 1987 General Election.

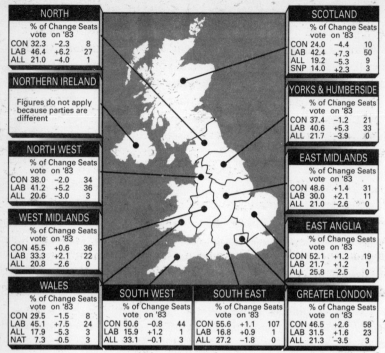

Figure 8.1 Voting behaviour of main geographic subgroups, showing change of parties' share from 1983 to 1987. (*Source*: *Sunday Times*, 14 June 1987; illustration by Geoff Sims)

Pollsters, politicians and pundits can compare political trends over time between groups of voters using the concept of 'swing', the psephological tool developed by Dr David Butler. It is calculated by subtracting the Conservative lead at one point in time, say the 1987 General Election, from another, say the 1983 General Election, and dividing by two (see Swing on p. 177). In layman's language, a swing of 2% would suggest that two people in a hundred had moved from one party to another. The swing figures between the elections are shown in the boxes for each geographical area in Figure 8.1. The base of the geographical analysis is the total number of votes cast in each region.

The demographic subgroups were calculated from a base of 23,396 electors in Britain interviewed by MORI during the election, weighted to the actual outcome. The availability of such a massive data base enabled us to estimate with reasonable confidence in the findings from relatively small groups within the electorate, such as young men and young women or working-class trade unionists and middle-class trade unionists.

Every subgroup, excepting Scotland, showed a decline in Labour's share. With the exception of the 18−24-year-old subgroup, every group showed an increase in Conservative support compared with when Labour last won power.

In Scotland, Labour's impressive showing between the 1983 and 1987 General Elections was represented by a swing of 7.5% from the Conservative share of the vote to Labour, which stemmed partly from a 5% decline in Alliance support. If the Labour Scottish performance had been replicated in England, the result would have been a hung Parliament instead of Mrs Thatcher being returned with a three-figure (101-seat) majority.

Labour had led the Tories by 3% when they last won office in 1974, but Mrs Thatcher reversed the Labour ascendancy to establish a seven point Conservative lead in May 1979, realizing a 5% swing. Labour's slight recovery, with a swing of 2.5% at this 1987 election was the result of a 1.5% swing in England, 7.5% in Scotland and a 5% swing from the Conservatives to Labour in Wales.

The decline in support for the Alliance parties was 3% in England, 5% in Scotland and 6% in Wales (with the swing calculation rounded to the nearest half per cent).

Among men, the Conservatives gained an 11% share between October 1974 and June 1987 at the same time that the Labour party lost 11%, a swing of 11% over the extended decade. Labour's success in attracting men back to its cause was unspectacular − only two points, while the Tories picked up one point for a mere half point swing.

Among women, a group targeted by the Labour campaign planners, the party did better, nearly halving the Conservatives' 1983 lead of 20% to 11%, a 4.5% swing. Another Labour target for recapture was the 18−24-year-olds, and the party's swing of 6% was among the most successful of all. Among the so-called 'Thatcher's Children' (those who have only been of

Portrait of the electorate

% of 1987 total voters		The 1983 vote			The 1987 vote		
		Con	Lab	Alin	Con	Lab	Alin
100	Total	44	28	26	43	32	23
49	Men	43	30	25	43	32	23
51	Women	46	26	27	43	32	23
14	18−24	42	33	32	33	40	21
19	25−34	40	29	29	39	33	25
33	35−54	44	27	27	45	29	24
34	55 +	47	27	24	48	31	21
23	Pensioner	51	25	23	47	31	21
19	AB-prof/managerial	60	10	28	57	14	28
24	C1-white collar	51	20	27	51	21	28
27	C2-skilled workers	40	32	28	40	36	22
30	DE-skilled workers	33	41	24	30	48	20
67	Owner occupier	52	19	28	50	23	25
23	Council tenants	26	47	24	22	56	19
7	Private tenants	41	33	23	39	37	21
7	Men 18−24	41	35	21	42	37	19
7	Women 18−24	42	31	25	31	42	24
9	Men 25−34	37	34	28	41	33	24
10	Women 25−34	42	25	30	37	33	27
16	Men 35−54	42	29	27	42	32	24
17	Women 35−54	46	24	28	47	27	25
17	Men 55 +	45	28	25	45	31	23
17	Women 55 +	49	26	24	46	32	20
9	Men 65 +	50	25	23	47	30	22
9	Women 65 +	51	25	23	46	33	20

4	Unemployed men	25	49	24	21	56	20
3	Unemployed women	32	41	24	23	54	19
17	North men	35	39	24	21	56	20
19	North women	40	33	25	33	41	22
13	Midland men	43	31	23	46	34	19
13	Midland women	46	27	24	45	29	24
19	South men	48	23	28	49	22	28
20	South women	51	18	30	51	24	24
	Home owners						
36	Middle class	58	12	29	57	15	28
31	Working class	46	25	27	43	32	23
	Council tenants						
2	Middle class	32	39	25	28	41	24
21	Working class	25	49	24	21	58	18
	Trade unions						
23	Members	31	39	29	30	42	26
15	Men	29	41	28	31	42	25
8	Women	34	34	31	29	41	27
3	18–24	31	34	23	29	46	23
5	25–34	29	37	32	28	47	23
10	35–54	30	40	29	29	40	29
5	55 +	32	40	26	36	37	24
10	ABC1	38	27	33	37	30	30
8	C2	27	44	27	28	47	24
5	DE	25	50	24	22	56	19
9	North	26	44	28	25	50	21
6	Midlands	32	40	25	35	39	24
8	South	35	32	32	33	34	32

Figure 8.2 Portrait of the electorate: how they voted in 1983 and 1987 according to various demographic subgroups. (*Source*: *Sunday Times*, 14 June 1987)

voting age under a government led by Mrs Thatcher), splitting the young men from the young women (Figure 8.2) shows that Labour's efforts were successful with the women, where it reversed an 11 point Tory lead in 1983 to an 11 point Labour lead in 1987. The 35—54 age group turned out to be the most sterile ground for Labour's campaign, where the swing was only a half of one per cent and where a massive 13 point drop since 1974 still remained.

Labour cut back a 20 point deficit in 1983 to 15% in 1987 among the over-55s, who represent a third of the electorate, but they still had a 9% gap to make up to get back to their 1974 winning level with this powerful voting group. Traditionally, pollsters have found that while the propensity to vote among 18—24-year-olds is barely half, more than 80% of the 55+ cohort turn out on polling day.

As with the younger women, Labour did better with older women than older men. The Alliance did better with younger women than men by a substantial 5% margin.

A majority of middle-class, ABC1, voters have traditionally voted for the Conservatives, varying little over the Thatcher decade. Labour did better in 1979, being only a point less than they were a decade earlier. The Alliance vote among the middle class held up between 1983 and 1987 somewhat better than among working-class respondents.

While in 1979, when Mrs Thatcher first gained power, 59% of the middle class voted Tory, in 1987 54% did. But the percentage of middle-class voters rose from 33 to 40% during the first Thatcher decade.

The middle classes turn out to vote on election day to a higher degree than do working class electors, accounting for the fact that of the voters in 1987, 42% were categorized as middle class.

The C2s, the battleground of the electorate, were the backbone of the Labour party's support in its years in power. Then a third of the voting public, their strength had been sapped to 27% by 1987, and at the same time Labour's share of their vote declined by a quarter. Nearly half of the larger base in 1974, 49%, voted Labour. It was little over a third this time.

In 1974 only one in five voted Tory, in 1987 it was two in five.

The unskilled workers and those living on state benefits and pension made up the DEs, nearly a third of the voting public. Labour's decline was less in this group and recovered somewhat in this last election, but it was still nine points off the 1974 level of Labour support.

The effect of the sales of council houses to sitting tenants, the cornerstone of the first Thatcher government's efforts to introduce popular capitalism to the working class, is shown by comparing working-class owner-occupier's voting patterns to those of working-class council tenants (see Figure 8.2). While among working-class homeowners the Conservatives had an 11 point lead, among working-class council tenants the Labour party had a massive 38 point lead, a 50 point difference between the two groups. In 1983 the figures were 21% Tory and 24% Labour respectively, so the gap widened between the two elections as the balance between them tilted as well.

In the days when Harold Wilson led the Labour party, more than half of trade union members supported the party of the trade unions; in 1987 only 42% did, up a mere 3% from the Labour's party's 1983 débâcle. In fact, among middle-class trade unionists, one in ten of the electorate, the Conservatives had a 7% lead and Labour tied with the Alliance at a 30% level of support compared to the Conservative's 37%.

In these figures are the evidence of the success of the 'Thatcher Revolution'.

The performance of the polls

Over the 13 General Elections since the war, and over the period of election polling, polls have performed, on average, about as would be expected from what we know about the science of sampling. The record of the polls in the 13 general elections since the war is shown in Table 8.3.

The margin of error on the gap should be double that of share, according to sampling theory, and indeed it is, according to the empirical evidence of 55 election forecasts over 42 years.

Table 8.3 Accuracy of the polls, 1945–1987

Year	Mean error gap	Average error per party	Number of of polls
	%	%	
1945	3.5	1.5	1
1950	4.6	1.7	3
1951	5.3	2.2	3
1955	0.2	0.9	2
1959	1.1	0.8	4
1964	0.8	1.5	4
1966	3.9	1.5	4
1970	6.6	2.2	5
1974 Feb	2.4	1.6	6
1974 Oct	5.0	1.6	6
1979	1.7	0.9	5
1983	4.3	1.1	6
1987	3.2	1.2	6
Average	3.3	1.4	55

About a quarter of the polls since 1945 have been able to estimate the Labour and Conservative share of the vote to within plus or minus 1%, and over 60% have forecast to within plus or minus 2%. These 55 polls have marginally underestimated the Tory share of the popular vote and marginally overestimated the Labour share. As polls do not measure postal voters and these are generally agreed to favour the Tories — perhaps by as much as 3 : 1 — the direction of these averages is not surprising.

Notes

1 Robert M. Worcester, 'A Poll Not Worth Two Cents', *The Times*, 26 January 1987.

9 Political Change in Britain: Ten Years of Thatcherism

The political triangle

The elements of political choice that determine the voting behaviour of the marginal voter, the swing voter who determines not only who wins but the size of the winning party's majority in the House of Commons, are principally three: the images attributed to each party as being seen to be fit to govern, united etc.; the image of the leadership of the parties as caring, understanding of the problems facing Britain and her role in the world, listening to the electorate etc.; and the perceived understanding and acceptance or consonance of the elector's ideas of the parties' stands on issues of importance or salience to the voter.

MORI's 'Agenda' poll for *The Times* taken on election day 1987 sought to measure the relative weight that the British electorate put on each of these factors, on a scale of zero to ten. On 11 June 1987 we found that 44% of the weight of the determinant was about policy, 35% about leader image and 21% about party image. Of course there was variation within the demography of the sample: Conservative voters were more leader-, less party-orientated and on the average for policy. Labour supporters were more party-, less policy-orientated and on the mean for leader, and Alliance supporters were more policy-, less leader(s)-orientated and average on party. Men were more concerned with policy, women with leaders; younger people were more policy-orientated, over-55s much more leader- and more party-conscious, and middle-class voters said they were more concerned with policy and working-class voters were more leader- and party-orientated.

I hypothesized at the time,[1] that as the measurement was taken at the apogee of the election battle, the scores would be much different at other times. To test this, we repeated the question four months later at the time of the 1987 Queen's Speech in November, and found very little change – none on the relative weight given to leadership, while the importance given to policies was 6% down and to the image of the leader 8% up. We have continued to monitor these factors and most recently, at the end of 1989, found once again only slight change, with leaders' image rated at 36% (up only 1% since the General Election), policies down 4%, to 40%, and party image changed the most, from 21% in 1987 to 24% in December 1989. None of these changes is statistically significant at the 95% confidence level, but they may change when leaders change or when a radically different political climate pertains.

In 1987, there was ample evidence that Labour did well on the caring issues while the Tories led on defence, law and order and in their ability to handle the economy. And while three-quarters of the electorate said they were satisfied with their standard of living and more people said it was higher then than five years earlier and was likely to be higher yet in another five years time under the Tories, the Conservative lead on inflation/prices/1economic competence remained. Yet by some nine to one there was agreement that 'the gap between the rich and the poor in Britain is too wide', indicating there were values held by the vast majority of the British public that questioned the Tory hegemony on the handling of the economy.

British values

Underlying these images and perceptions about issues and identification with parties are the values held by the aggregate electorate, made up of millions of individuals with differing backgrounds, levels of intelligence and affluence, educational advantages and aspirations and political consciousness. These values are perhaps the most difficult to identify and scale, segment and explain. But we use the tools we have, and do the best we can.

Over several years, Labour's share hung in the mid to upper thirties, through increasing unemployment, through the miners' strike, through the assassination attempt of Mrs Thatcher and into the run-up to the 1987 General Election. Despite a generally well-regarded election campaign in 1987, Labour's share fell to 32% on election day, rising afterwards once again to the 35–40% level, rarely lower, rarely higher, through to the end of 1988. Labour's share went down a bit, and up on occasion as high as 40%, and although many explanations were forthcoming, during that time Labour was never able to break through the 40% barrier for any sustained period.

At MORI we attempted to synthesize what 'values' people hold (see Figure 9.1, p. 114). We found in a survey in 1988 that over half, 54%, of the British public hold essentially socialist values while 39% are essentially 'Thatcherist'. It may be argued that these values are the real swing factors that win and lose elections, and that the sides of the triangle are really the facets of a tetrahedron, a three-sided solid, not a two-dimensional triangle, resting on a firm if hidden base of people's values. If this is so, and if the assumptions of the editor of the *New Statesman*, Stuart Weir, are correct ('the broad mass of people in this country are ready for a new progressive ideology which reconciles the British people's deep attachment to individualism with their still strong desire for social justice'), then why was Labour unable to do better?

We tested five pairs of concepts, using a technique originally developed by Professor Stephen Cotgrove; there may have been grounds for argument over the precise wording of the statements, but they reasonably described several relevant concepts on which most people have a view stemming from their own value system. It was a mark of comprehension among the sample that the level of 'don't know' was lower than average for conceptual questions, ranging from 5 to 8%.

BRITAIN TODAY

Attitudes and values in Thatcher's ninth year

MORI was commissioned by LWT's *Weekend World* programme in conjunction with the *Sunday Times*, to conduct a detailed assessment of attitudes to a wide range of social, economic and foreign affairs issues. The purpose of the survey was to ascertain the effects of nine years of Thatcherism on the values of the British people.

Fieldwork took place between 3–6 June among a representative quota sample of 1,030 adults aged 18 + at 102 constituency sampling points throughout Great Britain.

VOTING INTENTION

	11 June 1987	3–6 June 1987	Change
	%	%	+/–
Conservative	43	47	+4
Labour	32	40	+8
SLD]		7	–16
SDP	23	4	–19

SOCIALIST VS THATCHERIST VALUES

People have different views about the ideal society. This card shows a number of alternatives. Q.(1) Please read each pair of statements and then tell me which one, in each case, comes closest to you ideal – statement A or statement B. Q.(2) Now, for each pair of statements, please tell me whether you think statement A or statement B is most like Britain today?

	—— (1) ——			– (2) –	
	All	Con	Lab	SLD/SDP	All
	%	%	%	%	%
A. 'A mainly capitalist society in which private interests and free enterprise are most important'.	43	72	17	35	77
B. 'A mainly socialist society in which public interests and a more controlled economy are most important'.	49	25	76	57	17
A. 'A society which emphasises the social and collective provision of welfare'.	55	38	71	70	27
B. 'A society where the individual is encouraged to look after himself'.	40	59	25	26	66
A. 'A society which emphasises keeping people in work even where this is not very efficient'.	42	29	56	46	25
B. 'A society which emphasises increasing efficiency rather than keeping people in work'.	50	67	33	45	68
A. 'A society which allows people to make and keep as much money as they can'.	53	72	34	45	73
B. 'A society which emphasises similar incomes and rewards for everyone'.	43	26	61	48	19
A. 'A society in which the creation of wealth is more highly rewarded'.	16	25	9	9	75
B. 'A society in which caring for others is more highly rewarded'.	79	71	87	87	19

Values in Today's Britain

Thatcherist		Socialist
A society which allows people to make and keep as much money as they can	Ideal 53% / 43% 73% / 19%	A society which emphasises similar incomes and rewards for everyone
A society which emphasises increasing efficiency rather than keeping people in work	Actual 50% / 42% 68% / 25%	A society which emphasises keeping people in work even where this is not very efficient
A mainly capitalist society in which private interest and free enterprise are most important	43% / 49% 77% / 17%	A mainly socialist society in which public interests and a more controlled economy are most important
A society where the individual is encouraged to look after himself	40% / 55% 66% / 27%	A society which emphasises the social and collective provision of welfare
A society in which the creation of wealth is more highly rewarded	16% / 79% 75% / 19%	A society in which caring for others is more highly rewarded

ECONOMY

Q. The things people can buy and do – their housing, furniture, food, cars, recreation and travel – make up their standard of living. How satisfied or dissatisfied do you feel about your standard of living at present?

	All	Con	Lab	SLD/SDP
	%	%	%	%
Very satisfied	16]74	22]86	9]61	17]83
Fairly satisfied	58	64	52	66
Fairly dissatisfied	10]18	6]8	15]30	3]6
Very dissatisfied	8	2	15	3
Neither/don't know/ no opinion	8	6	9	11
Net satisfied	+56	+78	+31	+77

Q. Overall, do you think your present standard of living is higher, lower or about the same as five years ago?

	%	%	%	%
Higher	42	53	30	45
Lower	27	18	38	21
About the same	30	29	31	32
Don't know	1		1	
Net higher	+15	25	– 8	+24

Q. And do you think it will be higher, lower or about the same in five years time?

	%	%	%	%
Higher	35	48	24	31
Lower	23	11	34	27
About the same	33	33	33	35
Don't know	8	8	9	7
Net higher	+12	+37	–10	+4

Figure 9.1 MORI survey of 'Thatcherist' and 'Socialist' attitudes and values. (*Source: British Public Opinion*, July/August 1988)

More people in Britain said they believed the ideal society would be one which is a 'mainly socialist society in which public interests and a more controlled economy is more important' (49%), rather than 'a mainly capitalist society in which private interests and free enterprise are more important' (45%). Another surprising finding in terms of its strength in view of the times in which we live was that nearly eight people in ten (79%) favoured a 'society in which the caring for others is more highly regarded' rather than one in which the emphasis is on the creation of wealth.

Another set of important findings was that in every case, when asked for their view of Britain as it actually was, many of the public thought it was 'over the top'. On average, while seven people in ten saw Britain then as 'Thatcherist' (as we defined it), only four in ten wished it to be so. The discontinuity which emphasizes increasing efficiency rather than keeping people in work compared with Britain as they believe it to be under Mrs Thatcher. And the gap, ideal to actual, was as great as 59%, comparing rewarding caring with wealth creation.

But perhaps the biggest surprise in the survey's findings came when examining the dissonance or antimonies among supporters of the main political parties. We found that a third of those who said their voting intention 'if a general election were held today' was Labour held essentially Thatcherist values and over a quarter (27%) of those whose voting intention was Tory were essentially socialists, whether they knew it or not.[2]

The Thatcher decade of change

The 'Thatcher Decade' was a decade of change:[3] change in the composition of social class, change in housing, change in share ownership, change in trade union membership, change in industry and change in politics.

Class is important to an understanding of Britain and the British, and to politics in Britain. During the 1980s the social categorization of the British endured greater change than in any other decade in Britain's history. When Mrs Thatcher first took office in May 1979, one-third of the public were in the middle (ABC1) social class and two-thirds were in the working (C2DE) social class. A decade later, four in ten households are middle class, and six in ten working class, in political terms a 'swing' of 7% in the period of the Thatcher Revolution.

Housing change represented another part of the Thatcher Revolution over the decade. Mrs Thatcher's principal plank in her first-term programme of structural change was the sale of council houses to sitting tenants, and for tenants with significant tenure, at deep discounts. The degree to which this policy was successful is illustrated in the 16% swing over the period, from just over half the public, 52%, home owning in 1979 when Mrs Thatcher took office to two-thirds, 68%, by 1990. Most home owners are middle class, but a third of DEs, unskilled manual workers, are home owners as well. It was not lost on the Prime Minister that while Labour had a 25% lead over the Tories at the 1983 election among working-class council tenants, the Tories had a 21% lead among working-class home buyers. Indeed, in Thatcher's Britain home ownership is a better predictor of voting behaviour than class, although of course the two characteristics are correlated.

Another main tenet in the Thatcher programme of structural change has been the privatization programme which has taken share ownership in Britain from the bottom of the Western league tables to very near the top, from 7% of the public when the government changed hands in 1979 to some 22% in April–June 1990, a 15% swing, and among trade unionists, from 6%, a point less, to 24%, two points more.

Mainly as a result of the privatization programme, there are now a million fewer workers in the public sector than when Mrs Thacher first took office. Public sector employment at the beginning of the Thatcher era was 29% and 26% a decade later, a 3% swing. Many more are crossing over to the private sector in the Thatcher third term as a result of the privatizing of steel and water, with coal, electricity, property services and the railways (and more?) yet to come.

The steady Duke of York's march of trade union membership, from 24% of adults up to 30%, over 13 million members during the Wilson–Callaghan years, was reversed when Mrs Thatcher's trade union legislation took effect; trade union membership over the decade swung back 8%, to 22%, fewer than ten million members by the turn of the decade.

The structure of the trade union membership changed sharply as well, with the trade union movement by 1990 significantly more female, younger, and more middle class than a decade earlier. There has been an 8% swing to women, and towards middle-class members; a 9% swing away from the cloth-capped 'old Freds' of the 1960s and 70s; and three particularly marked swings:

- 16% swing to share owning among trade unionists;
- 30% swing to home owning; and
- 50% swing among trade unionists to being on the phone.

People believed then and now that 'Trade unions are essential to protect worker's interests' (88% then, and now), but while seven in ten people in 1978 believed that 'Trade unions have too much power in Britain today', in 1990 only a third (31%) do.

One unmistakable factor in all of this has been the massive destructuring of British industry over the period. In Labour's last full year of power, 1978, unemployment stood at under one-and-half million. During the Thatcher years it rose to over three million, and nearly 12% of the adult population were unemployed. Over the four years to 1990 the unemployment figures fell steadily until there were fewer than three million and under 10% unemployed, but with a rise forecast.

In 1981, Mrs Thatcher was the least popular Prime Minister. In the autumn of that year, only 25% of the public were satisfied with Mrs Thatcher's performance, while 62% were dissatisfied. The main thing that must have kept her going at the time was that the Labour leader, Michael Foot, with only 18% satisfied with his performance, was the least popular party leader since the war. The Tories were three points ahead of Labour in 1978, which would have produced a hung Parliament if it had been replicated at the General Election that most observers expected Prime Minister Callaghan to call in 1978. But he did not, and in June 1979 Mrs Thatcher led the Tories to a 45% to 38% victory over Labour to begin the most revolutionary decade in Britain's history.

Notes

1　Robert M. Worcester, 'Swings and Falls that Spawned a Landslide', *The Times*, 13 June 1987.
2　Robert M. Worcester, 'Polls Apart', *New Socialist*, Summer 1988.
3　Robert M. Worcester, in *Decade of Revolution* (Adam Smith Institute).

Part III
Methodological and
Other Considerations

10 Introduction

The presentation of the findings of public opinion surveys or polls in the media has three principal functions: reporting (explaining what is going on); analytical (why what is happening is happening); and thirdly (and least effective in my view), predictive (trying to forecast who is going to win). In an effort to help the reader to understand the uses − and limitations − of public opinion polls, this section of the book is offered.

It is offered to any editor, journalist or commentator who recognizes the potentially valuable contribution poll findings can make to a deeper understanding of a story, or who acknowledges that journalistic training does not necessarily make one an accomplished pollster; to any academic or student of political or social behaviour who wants to understand one of the most accurate and useful tools available to the social sciences; or to the politician who needs to understand how these infernal machines which the media use to pummel him with are constructed; or to the businessman or woman who wants to know more about how consumers and shareholders, pressure group activists and the public are measured; or to the reader who is just curious to know more about polling.[1]

One of the first of the guidebooks to polls and polling, and still one of the best, was the late, great, George Gallup's *The Sophisticated Poll Watcher's Guide*;[2] also worth a look are Leo Bogart's *Polls and the Awareness of Public Opinion*, originally published as *Silent Politics*,[3] and Roll and Cantril's *Polls: Their Use and Misuse in Politics*.[4]

This section of this present book is not a 'do-it-yourself' guide; it is not a treatise on sampling theory or questionnaire construction or applied multivariate analytical techniques. That is the role of a more extensive text, and the really interested are recommended to look to the *Consumer Market Research Handbook*[5] for detailed guidance. Here I aim to give a simple explanation of how we do what we do and how we do it together with suggestions as to how journalists might follow a few principles which would ensure that their readers, listeners or viewers were better served by their newspapers or broadcasts, and guidance for readers or viewers so that they might understand better the reports of poll findings.

A great deal has been written about polls and their publication, wise and foolish, thoughtful and thoughtless, sense and non-sense. In the Bibliography there is an extensive list of the literature of polling, and yet it but scratches the surface and suffers, admittedly, from an Anglo-American bias. One reason for this is that polling is largely an American invention; it is also perhaps most used (and probably misused) in the United States. The language of the polling fraternity, which now numbers in tens of thousands those following the trades of opinion polling and its twin sisters, attitude research and marketing research, is English. So if you are interested further, beyond the few pages here presented, go to the literature; better yet, go to the experts. In every Western country, indeed, in every developed and in many less well-developed countries in the world, there are well-educated, well-trained researchers in private firms, government agencies and in the universities who will go out of their way to be of help to the journalist or commentator or member of the public who seeks guidance about technique on the one hand or information about findings on the other. The assistance is there for the asking and is part of the open tradition of the pollster's trade.

Pollsters have a great deal of power in democratic societies. Witness the attention now given in Eastern Europe to the polls now being conducted there. When the Berlin Wall cracked, and *glasnost* took hold, one of the many manifestations of the new openness was the springing up of survey research firms in the Eastern European countries and the publication in the East and the West of poll findings. In MORI's first tentative adventures across the former Iron Curtain, we were pleased and surprised to find how responsive people were to our inquiries. It was if they had been waiting to talk to the world via our interview. Response rates are very nearly 100%; street interviews found people queuing to answer the questions on our clipboards. When the British Foreign Office provided grants for politicians from Poland, Hungary and the other Eastern European countries to visit Britain to see how British democracy works, they arranged for them to see the Houses of Parliament, to meet members of the political parties, to visit the Foreign Office itself, and provided a slot in the visitors' busy week to visit MORI for a two-hour lecture and question-and-answer session on the role of opinion research in a democratic society.

Reporting polls: raison d'être

In every newspaper and every news bulletin, in many columnists' and pundits' comments, frequently in the editorial 'thunderings' of leader writers, are references to public opinion. Politicians speak with confidence of the views of the public. Pressure groups convey to anyone who will listen the views of those they purport to represent, sometimes multiplying a hundredfold those they really represent. Every dinner party conversation, every pub talk, every speech to a Woman's Institute or National Farmers' Union local meeting is sprinkled with such references. 'Everybody knows that . . .', 'The public's view on that is . . .', 'What people are thinking is . . .', 'Public opinion won't have it!', is to be heard throughout the land. Indeed, soon after the East–West breakthrough in Germany Chancellor Kohl of the Federal Republic spent an uncomfortable day or so misrepresenting East German public opinion on the issue of the German border with Poland, under the mistaken impression that the mass of East German opinion was not content to respect the Polish border when in fact 89% of East Germans were. Kohl quickly turned on the issue and a diplomatic gaffe which might have delayed the progress of reunification was averted.

Sometimes 'public opinion' is the extension of the journalist's own prejudices, sometimes of the political hack's taxi driver/lift operator *vox populi* report; sometimes the result of a pressure group or political party's (usually ineffective) effort to manipulate a bandwagon or a backlash, sometimes of an unrepresentative phone-in or questionnaire-in-the-magazine mail-in poll, or a newspaper's 'straw poll'; or, increasingly frequently, it can be the outcome of a scientifically conducted, properly reported, professionally constructed public opinion poll which carries with it the best combination of polling expertise and journalistic excellence in providing a 'state-of-the-art' effort to report, explain, entertain and educate the reader/listener/viewer with the most accurate, up-to-date, measure of public opinion.

Anyone can sound public opinion. In Athenian Greece it was done with demos, but only the tiny elite had a say; in the eighteenth century the Frenchman J. Hector St John de Crevecoeur travelled the American colonies probing the public mood;[6] in the nineteenth century the first newspaper poll was taken in America while Disraeli's 'Tadpole and Tapers' went among the electorate in order to gauge the voters' mood.[7] Each President since Roosevelt, each Prime Minister since Macmillan has had his (or her) pollster. Polls were published in pre-war America, Australia, Britain, Germany, France and Japan. Over the years some politicians used them, some were scared of them, but few ignored them. Some papers employ sophisticated and serious polling efforts in an attempt to extend the reach of excellence in journalism, others, mainly popular papers, women's magazines, pop radio stations and breakfast television shows, treat polls as a game, with more interest in their value as entertainment than for public education or even honest reporting.

News outlets commission their own polls and take elaborate care and go to great expense to employ top polling organizations to design and conduct them and some then turn the data over to inexperienced writers who consider the assignment an imposition, the requirement to liaise with the pollster a burden, the deadline for copy imminent, the use of graphics redundant and the sub-editing and headline writing beyond their control. Yet in commissioning a poll the editor has authorized one of the most expensive and complex forms of journalism known. Too often the education and training the journalist received omitted any passing reference to statistics or even basic mathematics or graphical representation; some countries' educational systems develop either the innumerate literates, or the illiterate numerates, people who can spell and punctuate but not do percentages, or who can calculate but not write.

Frequently, instead of developing a journalist who is interested in polls into a specialist writer, editors will assign a political writer to write up election polls, a medical correspondent to write up a poll on, for example, concern about AIDS, a women's page writer to by-line a piece about attitudes to sex and morality, and a sports writer to write about people's interest in football. There is a case for input from the specialist writer to be sure, but far better is for the poll to be handled by a journalist trained in the intricacies of polling who can call on the qualified pollster on the one hand and the specialist writer/section editor on the other to squeeze the most news and insight out of the expenditure on the poll.

Far, far worse in practice, is the sometimes careless secondary reporting of poll data. Even news media who go to great efforts to report thoroughly and responsibly their own commissioned polls will sometimes pick up the results of 'voodoo (i.e. unrepresentative) polls' and report them as gospel, or take the files of foreign correspondents who, not knowing any better, report polls taken weeks before an election as predictions of the outcome.

I define an 'opinion poll' as a 'survey of the attitudes of a representative sample of a defined population'. In other words, not 'voodoo polls' such as the 'Special *Sun* Survey' on 'The Young Divorcees' or other papers' polls which get readers to write in with their views and then report them dressed up as real polls complete with statistics, graphs and jargon. I remember in the early days of Victor Matthews when the *Daily Express* had the idea of putting a ballot in the paper – hoping maybe

10 or 15,000 people would write in to give their views. On this basis, the *Express* thought, the poll would be ten or 15 times better (that is bigger) than a MORI poll (and a lot cheaper). Over 70,000 people returned a ballot and some 63,000 of them said they would vote Tory if there were a general election. Their 'poll' under represented *Express*-reading Labour supporters by a factor of eight.[8]

Other things that happen too often include:

- Long-range projections: reports of polls more than weeks or even months before an election or even before an election is announced with 'Poll indicates Labour (or Tory or Alliance) to win by a landslide'. It didn't.
- Misleading headlines: sharp swings or significant leads suggested from insignificant differences in the poll.
- Decimal points: statistical spurity, suggesting a higher degree of accuracy than is possible with polls. Polls at best can only be approximations, accurate to plus or minus 1 or 2%.
- Secondary reporting: leaving out who did the poll, when it was done, etc.
- Misleading graphics: inaccurate, miscalculated bar charts, wrongly spaced trend lines, squeezed spacing to emphasize change, misproportioned pie charts etc.
- Paraphrasing questions: it is vital to know precisely how questions were phrased in order to be able to judge any bias, leading of the respondent, or 'inappropriate' language, such as words not in common use, jargon or technical phrases.
- Unknown pollsters: one telephone poll of 200 people, during the British 1983 General Election, treated seriously only by the *Morning Star*, was done in the Prime Minister's constituency of Finchley by a Middlesex Polytechnic lecturer which forecast Mrs Thatcher would lose her seat by a 42% to 27% margin. (You will have noticed she didn't.)
- Phone-in polls: such as ABC's infamous telephone phone-in the evening of the first Carter–Reagan debate, or worse, BBC Radio Four's 'contribution' to the debate on hanging

when listeners were invited to phone one number to vote 'yes' and another to vote 'no' – one listener, Desmond, phoned 157 times, 28 no's, 2 yes's and 127 disenfranchised (rather than 'don't know') because the lines were engaged. The yes's won, 52% to 48%, and this was reported as serious news on the BBC's 'The World Tonight' (another case of secondary reporting).

- Putting words into pollsters' mouths: at the 1987 General Election one political editor reported 'pollsters expect the pro-Alliance trend to speed up in the final two days before polling'. MORI did not say that at the time, neither did Gallup, nor did NOP and I do not know of any other pollster who did.

- Politicians' comments on polls: MPs do not get high marks for sincerity when it comes to commenting on poll results. On the one hand they point with enthusiasm to poll findings which support them or their views, and on the other rubbish those polls that show them losing support or espousing an unpopular cause.

- Bogus polls: papers often pick up bogus polls as if they were properly conducted. During the Darlington by-election in March 1983 the Conservative candidate, Michael Fallon, released a Young Conservatives' straw poll to *The Times* who published it. Fallon then had it published himself, declaring it in a leaflet delivered to voters' homes to be 'a poll, reported in *The Times*' as if it were a real poll. It showed a 14.5% (sic) Conservative lead. They lost by 6%.

On this last point, the Conservatives are by no means the only culprits in Britain ever to use polls and canvass returns to try to manipulate voters. In the 1983 General Election, in the Westbury constituency a Liberal leaflet purported to show their candidates, David Hughes, just 2% behind the Conservatives, and 'fast catching up'. On election day the Tory candidate Dennis Walters had a majority 8,506, or 14%.

Perhaps the SDP booby prize should go to Gary Halliwell in Westminster North. There a local leaflet showed two sets of figures under the headline 'Alliance second and gaining'.

It showed the SDP reducing a 12 point Tory lead over Halliwell to just four points in the space of a week. On election day Halliwell came third with a mere 15.7 per cent of the vote, while Labour failed by only 1,710 votes to wrest the seat from the Conservatives. And Labour supporter Peter Kellner, then political editor of the *New Statesman*, ended a piece on 'How party polls were used to mislead voters' with the following PS: 'Honesty compels us to acknowledge receiving a letter from John Tilley, a Liberal councillor in Kingston, who tells us that a local Labour leaflet claimed: "Fact. Our canvass returns in Kingston show that 33 per cent of the voters are solidly behind Labour." On 9 June, Labour came third with 12.2 per cent; its local candidate lost his deposit.' And the *Scotsman*'s former editor, Chris Baur, on the basis of the various parties' canvass returns in one by-election predicted a record turnout of approximately 150%, by adding up the parties' claims of support.

In the United States, on the Saturday night before the Tuesday primary the then Senator William Fulbright announced that his private polls showed him ahead by two to one. A few days later Dale Bumpers, his opponent, won the election by a margin of 55%/45%. Later Fulbright's aides admitted that there were no private polls taken.

As indicated above, I define an opinion poll as 'a survey of the opinions of a representative sample of a defined population'. The words 'representative sample' are an essential part of the equation, yet there seem to be an increasing number of questionable surveys being conducted by various programmes and publications, especially women's magazines. They are representative of nothing except the views of those people who read the magazine, tear the page out, tick the boxes, address the envelope, then post it.

One example involved the magazine *Options*. It turned out that 29% of the respondents to their questionnaire were *Guardian* readers. Since approximately 3% of the women in Britain read the *Guardian*, there were approximately ten times as many *Guardian* readers in the sample as there should have been if the results were representative of the adult female population of this country. To be fair, *Options* magazine did not stretch credulity too far in reporting the survey. The real damage was done by newspaper and radio reports, which left out all the caveats about the unrepresentative nature of the sample, merely stating: 'A new survey out today reports that . . .'! The findings of such 'surveys' are then absorbed into our national consciousness.

A Reuters report published in the *International Herald Tribune* on 3 May 1984 reported: 'The French Socialist Party will (sic) win 22% of the vote in elections for the European Parliament next month, according to an opinion poll published on Wednesday by the Sofres Organisation in the rightist newspaper *Le Figaro*.' Now there is no opinion poll in the world that, taken in April, can predict the outcome of an election held on 14 June, and that goes for France, Britain, or anywhere else in the Western world. A poll is representative of opinion only at the time it is taken.

At an even lower common denominator, public opinion is measured by a politician whose postbag tells him what people think. During the early days of the Falklands crisis, a former Cabinet minister proclaimed authoritatively in the House of Commons that 'Public opinion in Britain is swinging massively against the war'. The evidence, he said, was that several hundred letters had been sent to him, nearly all of which had expressed their opposition to the government's actions in sending the Task Force to the Falklands. The politician was Tony Benn. The question is: just how representative were those letters? How reliable was his sample? But Benn also has said 'If you deny people knowledge of what the community is thinking then those who think those thoughts believe they are out of line'.

Lucifer (Harry Henry) writing in *Admap* under the title 'We, the people of England . . .',[9] reported

the Southend *Evening Echo* carried a coupon asking its readers' opinions on the liberalization of Sunday trading. Some 2.5 per cent of the coupons were returned – most of them, inevitably with a self-selected sample in such a field, opposed to the idea. On the basis of this piece of nonsense the Editor, a Mr Jim Worsdale, has concluded that although a response such as this may not be fully representative, it is a fair guide to public feeling and has taken it upon himself to write to local MPs, councils and chambers of trade 'to let them know the outcome' of what he refers to as 'a democratic exercise'. One cannot help feeling that he and his kidney would look a little less absurd if they confined themselves to reporting the winners of the local Women's Institute cake competitions, for which at least they are trained.

Lucifer's title, 'We, the people of England ...', comes from a well-known English anecdote which was quoted by Professor Thomas A. Bailey, author of *The Man in the Street*, and is cited in George Gallup's *The Sophisticated Poll Watcher's Guide*:

The 'pressure boys' have perfected techniques for making noise all out of proportion to the numbers of their constituents, and in so doing, they provide another example of the 'tyranny of the minority'. Clever operatives can stir up a tremendous pother, particularly when they assail their congressman with padded petitions, 'parrot' letters, and form telegrams signed with names lifted from the telephone directory. The nervous legislator, ever anxious for his seat, may easily be misled by the aggressive minority that deluges him with telegrams, while the great and apathetic majority tends to its daily diversions. He may be unduly impressed when a man whom he has never heard of appears as the alleged spokesman for 22,000,000 people. The congressman in such circumstances would do well to remember the three tailors of Tooley Street, who, in addressing a petition to the King, began, 'We the people of England ...'[10]

Raison d'etre? As Leo Bogart put it:

Public misunderstanding of opinion surveys can be expected to continue as long as the mass media ignore or belittle their technical intricacies. This attitude may be the inevitable result of regarding the raw percentages of yes and no votes, rather than the interpretation of their meaning, as the essential product of polling. Inevitably the news media must show greater interest not just in the results of opinion surveys, but in the broader application of social research and social theory to the large and complex subjects out of which specific news stories emerge each day.[11]

Notes

1   This section was originally developed for a 'Journalist's Guide to the Publication of Opinion Survey Results', a private monograph which has been widely distributed to journalists, editors (all national newspaper editors were sent a copy just before the 1987 General Election) and lecturers and students. It has been translated into several other languages. Its immediate precursor was the *Newsroom Guide to Polls and Surveys*, by G. Cleveland Wilhoit and David H. Weaver of the Bureau of Media Research, School of Journalism, Indiana University, USA, for the American Newspaper Publishers Association (Washington, DC, 1980). I am grateful for permission from Wilhoit and Weaver to use some of their examples and ideas and for being allowed to quote freely from their useful work.

2   George Gallup, *The Sophisticated Poll Watcher's Guide* (Princeton University Press, 1976).

3   Leo Bogart, *Silent Politics: Polls and the Awareness of Public Opinion* (John Wiley, 1972). Reprinted as *Polls and the Awareness of Public Opinion* (Transaction Books, 1986).

4   Charles W. Roll and Albert H. Cantril, *Polls: Their Use and Misuse in Politics* (Seven Locks Press, Cabin John, 1972).

5   Robert M. Worcester and John Downham (eds), *Consumer Market Research Handbook*, 3rd edn (Elsevier North Holland, 1986).

6   J. Hector St John de Crevecoeur, *Letters from an American Farmer* (Signet Classic, 1963).

7   Benjamin Disraeli, *Sybil* (Oxford University Press, 1981).

8   Robert M. Worcester, 'A Pollster's View of How the Press Uses Survey Results', in *UK Press Gazette*, 16 September 1985.

9   Lucifer, 'We, The People of England', in *Admap*, January 1986.

10   Gallup, *The Sophisticated Poll Watcher's Guide, op. cit.*

11   Bogart, *Silent Politics, op. cit.*

11 The Art of Asking Questions

The title of this chapter[1] is taken from the title of a little book first published in 1951 by a wise practitioner of the art, Stanley Payne, and which is now in its thirteenth printing. There is probably no more useful — and at the same time entertaining — book that the novice opinion researcher, or journalist or other interested student of opinion surveys, could consult. Journalists, perhaps justifiably, think themselves expert at asking questions. But think of the type of question they all too often ask: 'Well, it looks like Labour is going to win, doesn't it?' My favourite question was put to the British public in 1938: 'Are you in favour of direct retaliatory action against Franco's piracy?[2] In those 11 words, five rules of good question construction were broken.

1 Ask balanced questions: 'Do you favour or oppose . . .?'
2 Define your terms: one man's direct retaliatory action is a punch on the nose; another's is a nuclear bomb.
3 Use language in common usage: 'retaliatory' would likely be misunderstood by many people, especially in 1938.
4 Explain who's who: MORI questions nearly always say, 'Mrs Thatcher, the Prime Minister' or 'George Bush, President of the United States of America', or 'Nelson Mandela, the black ANC leader' (in a poll in South Africa).
5 Eschew pejoratives: 'Piracy' — what was surprising was that the poll found 22% who were against taking action with a loaded question like that one!

Wilhoit and Weaver's *Newsroom Guide*[3] gives an excellent layman's outline to evaluating survey questions, which I have drawn on with their permission in the section below. For further information on questionnaire construction see chapter 5 of the *Consumer Market Research Handbook.*[4]

Detecting question bias

What may appear at first examination to be negligible differences in word choice in a survey question may give strikingly different results. In fact, the differences can be so great that one survey researcher in the United States came up with what he called the 'dog whistle theory' of questioning. That is, the person interviewed often 'hears' the difference in questions when the researcher doing the study does not.

Numerous examples support the point. When two survey research firms asked about happiness using slightly different questions, they found surprising differences in answers. Beginning with similar introductory statements about how happy survey respondents were, Gallup and the National Opinion Research Centre (NORC) asked of Americans:

(Gallup) Are you very happy? Are you fairly happy? or, Are you not very happy?

(NORC) Are you very happy? Are you pretty happy? or Are you not too happy?

The only difference between the questions is use of the words 'fairly', 'pretty', and 'not too'; yet the percentage differences between the questions is dramatic. About 15% more persons report they are very happy when the question is phrased as Gallup asked it.

More serious examples may be found in politics. The *Washington Post* published a dramatic example of how question wording affects something as mercurial as presidential popularity. In a national telephone survey of about 1,500 adults, the

Post compared the results of three presidential job performance questions.

Gallup has asked this question for about 40 years:

> Do you approve or disapprove of the way [President's name] is handling his job as President?

Harris asks the question this way:

> How would you rate the job [President's name] is doing as President? Would you say he is doing an excellent, pretty good, only fair or a poor job?

The *Post* asked a third question:

> Suppose you were to grade President [name] A, B, C, D, or F for the way he is handling his job as President. What grade would you give him?

The results showed dramatically the truth of the maxim that what you ask is what you get. The Gallup question gave the most favourable view of the President, probably because the two choices are extremes. Many persons apparently are hesitant to say they disapprove, even though they may not actually approve. The Harris question provided the least favourable view of the President, partly because Harris Associates interpret 'only fair' as being unfavourable. The *Post*'s questions resulted in a middle-ground of response, but it, too, suffers from the ambiguity of what people mean when they answer 'C'.

The point is that one should be wary of drawing results from a measure of public opinion based on data from any single question, without looking carefully at the question wording.

Problems with questions

Stanley Payne was right 40 years ago when he termed survey questioning an art. More importantly, these results show that people listen to questions with greater care than some have conceded. The lesson is that journalists, with their critical eye for words and word usage, should pay particularly close attention to survey questions when they are reporting results and their readers should look to the journalist to publish the question *exactly* the way it was asked. Too often the careless journalist or overly parsimonious sub-editor will shorten or paraphrase a question to give the reader the information that would suggest that an unbalanced or, even worse, biased question was asked. The most common, and often unwittingly edited, type of question is asked as, for example, 'Do you favour or oppose a return to capital punishment?' and reported as 'Do you favour a return to capital punishment?' or worse, 'Do you favour the death penalty?' or even worse, not reprinting the question asked at all but reporting '78% say bring back hanging'.

Here are some tips on what to look for in questions:

(1) Are they clear? Read the question aloud. If you have forgotten the point by the time you get to the end, or if you stumble over the words, the chances are others did. Clarity is not usually a problem with the major national pollsters, but studies done for interest groups often have fuzzy questions, sometimes deliberately. *Doonsbury*, the cartoon strip, recently mocked 'advocate' polls showing a tobacco industry spokesman being interviewed saying: '. . . and a national survey, commissioned especially for the tobacco industry, found that a majority of Americans do *not* support more restrictive anti-tobacco measures!'. The interviewer, pointing out that the findings were contradictory to other poll findings, reads out the question: 'Do you favour gestapo-style police tactics to prevent smoking in public?' 'Oh sure, we could quibble over question wording,' is the spokesman's reply.

(2) Does the question ask for a dual response? All too often a question will be drafted to which a respondent can perfectly properly respond: 'Yes, *and* no.' For example: 'Do you favour or oppose bringing back the death penalty for premeditated murder and life sentences for manslaughter?' The question asks at least two, possibly four, questions. A respondent may say that he does favour both the one and the

other, or the other but not the one, but he may also favour the death penalty for both offences or oppose both or even, possibly if perhaps illogically, favour the death penalty for manslaughter (possibly because he does not understand the word) and oppose it for murder.

(3)   Is the question precise? A good survey question says precisely what object the item refers to, leaving no room for ambiguity. Here is an example of a problem question: 'Did you happen to vote in the last election?' The question is incomplete in that it fails to tell the respondent which election; for example, asked of a respondent in mid 1990, was it the last General Election (in 1987), the last local election, (in 1990), or even the last European Parliament election (in 1989), which for a third of the country, those not living in areas where there was a local election in May 1990, was the last election in the area in which they live?

(4)   Is the time period defined? The period over which the question is related may be crucial to the respondent's answer. Time is a difficult concept for many people. For example: 'Did you go abroad last year?' As well as possibly being imprecise as to whether travel was on business or on holiday, does 'last year' refer to the previous calendar year, the 12 months back from when the question was asked, or even, for those at or with children at school, the school year?

(5)   Is the question loaded? Reputable pollsters have too much at stake in their work to be caught intentionally biasing a question. Special interest groups, however, sometimes have a vested interest in loading a question to get a certain result, as the *Doonsbury* cartoon points out. Blatant loading is easy to spot, but subtle loading, intentional or unintentional, may be less easy. Did you notice the subtle loading in the examples on the death penalty above? Use of the phrase 'return to' reminds the respondent that for many years Britain had the death penalty and that it would not necessarily be 'bad form' to agree or favour something that went before.

One of the worst examples Wilhoit and Weaver quote is from a poll commissioned by a rocket propellant corporation to convince the US Congress that there was massive public sentiment for the space programme: 'The US and the Russians are locked in a tense struggle for control of outer space. Do you favor increased expenditures for the US space program?'[5] How could one say 'No' to such a question?

(6) Does the question assume knowledge on the part of the respondent which he or she might not have? Another common error in survey questions is assuming the respondents know something about what the question asks, with a resulting distortion of the extent and direction of public opinion. Questions about opinion toward future legislation or even pending legislation provide excellent examples. For instance: 'In general, do you agree or disagree with the proposals outlined in the Chancellor's Budget Speech yesterday?'

(7) Does the question ask for a comparison that is meaningful to the respondent? If a question asks for the respondent to compare something he or she knows, but then asks for a comparison to something unknown, the resulting answer would be meaningless. For instance, 'Do you think that the Community Charge or Poll Tax that you are being asked to pay is fair in light of what other local authorities are charging?' This question assumes a lot; not only that they know the level of their own poll tax but they have a basis of comparison that is meaningful. It may well be that the respondent has a view on this related to what the respondent paid last year in local rates, but has no idea of how it compares with other local authorities.

(8) Is the question's meaning obscured by asking about a very complicated behaviour in simplistic terms? This happens to the best of pollsters. For example: 'Where do you usually get most of your news about what's going on in the world today – from the newspapers or radio or television or talking to people or where?' Without knowing what type of news, it is hard to argue that this question has much meaning. Fashion news for the modern professional or business woman may come from a woman's magazine while her business news comes from the *Financial Times* and *The Economist* and her main source of national news is watching ITN's *News at Ten*. This is the type

of question most often asked in the 'voodoo' phone-in polls so favoured by the popular papers and local radio.

(9) Does the question use a balanced scale? My colleagues and I became interested in the bias inherent in unbalanced scales over a decade ago when a United States Information Agency official insisted on using unbalanced scales and inappropriate language (for Britain) in a multi-country survey of so-called 'elite' opinion. To test our hypothesis, we carried out an extensive pilot test of the language they proposed to force upon us, which we later reported in a paper presented to a professional conference.[6]

Instead of using balanced scales with verbal tags — such as: agree strongly; agree; neither agree nor disagree; disagree; disagree strongly; or: very satisfied; fairly satisfied; fairly dissatisfied; very dissatisfied — they used: very great; considerable; some; little; very little. Those who answered 'some' overlapped with 'little' and 'considerable', and those who answered 'little' overlapped with both 'some' and 'very little'. They also used the word 'quite' which has a very different meaning in American English from British usage.

(10) Is it a 'Yes/No' question asking for an attitude? We virtually never ask bi-polar questions other than for factual or behavioural matters, such as 'Do you normally wear glasses for reading?' In general, any question that has a Yes/No answer is likely to inflate the favourable response to an item, regardless of whether the question itself is loaded. But, a more subtle form of loading combines prestige attachment or social desirability with a tendency toward yea-saying on the part of some respondents.

Colleagues at MORI produced a paper in 1976[7] to test the hypothesis that the British public tended to be more likely to give an affirmative answer to a question put to them in a positive way than a negative answer to a negative question. They found, in Britain at least, strong evidence of yea-saying. On three statements tested, the percentage agreeing with the positive wording exceeded that of those disagreeing with the comparable negative wording by at least 6% and in one case up to 19%. The negative wording was also found to be generally more difficult for respondents to comprehend, as shown by the larger 'Don't Know' response.

(11) Are appropriate filter questions asked? There is little point in asking petrol purchase questions of someone who, although they may drive, does not usually buy the petrol for the family car, or the brand of tinned soup when the respondent never sees the label and does not know which brand because he (usually) doesn't make the purchase decision.

(12) Are questions asked to get at intensity of feeling? Typically, opinion questionnaires are quite thorough in getting at direction or feeling (pro, con, or neutral) about political issues. Often, though, effective public opinion — that is, the version of public opinion most listened to by policymakers — is more accurately reflected in how strongly, or intensely, people feel about the issues. A good case in point is the issue of Sunday trading. Over the years, surveys we and others have done have shown overwhelming public opinion in favour of stores being allowed to trade on Sunday. Yet, when the House of Commons was given a free vote on this issue, the strength of feeling of minority groups was so well marshalled to lobby against the measure that it was defeated.

The means by which questions are tested by conscientious researchers is to try them out on their colleagues first, then on members of the public in a pilot test. Respondents are asked the question first, with the researcher listening carefully for the response or any questions arising. The respondent is then asked what he or she meant by their answer and what is their understanding of the question. Finally split-ballot techniques are employed, asking matched samples different versions of questions being tested, such as those utilized in the experiments noted above. (See also 'Piloting', below.)

There are still more problems with questions to be borne in mind. For example, is there a position bias, an order effect? Placement of survey questions in a certain order may bias overall results. For example, asking first how a respondent thinks most people feel about a certain issue may affect the way the person responds to a later question about how he or she personally feels about the issue.

When detecting possible question order bias, one should always ask whether the researcher was aware of the potential problem. Alternating or changing question order may have been used to minimize such bias. It can also be tested using the split-ballot technique described above.

Another point to consider is whether anything affected the responses at the time of the fieldwork. The technical details which should accompany every substantive poll report will give the specific dates when interviewing was conducted. These dates should be checked to see if breaking news may have affected all or part of the survey results. For example, if the Prime Minister makes a strong, highly visible decision during the time interviewers are in the field asking people how well they feel she is doing her job, the survey results may be dramatically affected by the Prime Minister's action.

One important key to evaluating survey questions is to find out who sponsored the study. In most cases that information is explicit, but if it is not, the reporter has not done his or her job in reporting the poll story and should have dug until that knowledge was made public. Knowing the axe is being ground by the sponsor of the study will provide leads on where to look for question bias, even if the survey is actually carried out by a reputable firm. One way to evaluate specific questions is to try to put oneself 'in the shoes' of the respondent, looking for problems of question sequence and meaning.

It is important to find out whether prompts or showcards were used. Some years ago Marplan polled for the *Guardian* newspaper. In asking their respondents 'What is the most important problem facing the country?', they used a showcard and asked people to select from a list. Unfortunately, when the list was derived the issue of strikes and industrial relations was not included, it not being a particular problem at the time. Several months later, the miners' strike was on, filling the television screens and the front pages of the national newspapers every day. MORI's 'most important problem' question, asked open-ended, i.e. without a prompt list, showed strikes soaring as a problem, yet it did not appear in the *Guardian*'s reports.

Another consideration is the method of interviewing. Was the interviewing carried out in person, face to face, or over the telephone, by post or by some other means? Some question formats – such as aided-recall requiring visual examples – can be used only in face-to-face settings. Others may be useful with all forms of interviewing.

George Gallup developed an approach to questioning in the 1940s which many researchers could do well to emulate today. He described it as his 'quintadimensional approach', since it probes five aspects of opinion.:

1 The respondent's awareness and general knowledge about the subject.
2 His/her overall opinion.
3 The reasons the views are held.
4 Specific views on specific aspects of the problem.
5 Intensity with which the views are held

He also warned about the literal-minded respondent, citing a Canadian experience of asking a farmer his length of residence: 'Twenty-six feet, six inches' was the precise reply.

For the reasons outlined above, we rarely ask 'Yes/No' questions when attempting to assess opinions or attitudes. Nearly always, attitude or opinion questions can be finely graded into measures of shades of opinion, with improved precision, by the use of rating scales. Yet journalists and editors frequently suggest that 'Yes/No' type questions be asked, and when offered a more informative, better detailed understanding of the public's intensity of feeling on an issue, push to collapse scale results back into a two-answer framework.

Another question technique often used in attitude and marketing research but less frequently in the pressure cooker of political polls is the probing question: 'Why do you say that?', 'What caused you to take that view?' and 'What do you think might be done?' – three lead-on's from attitudinal questions that allow the respondent to express in his own words his views, feelings and attitudes, answers being recorded verbatim by the interviewer and analysed by the researcher to 'put flesh on to the statistical bones' of the data.

In the field of opinion research, the pollster is often caught between the rock of the editor/journalist, who is most interested in 'the score' of who is ahead or behind in the election or how many times a week in a sex poll, and the hard place of the serious reader, frequently an academic who believes that the newspaper's expenditure on data from survey research should be almost entirely descriptive or diagnostic as a public service.

There are trade-offs to be made between the two. 'Score' questions, so loved by the popular press, are usually cheap and cheerful, two-dimensional, readily adapted to a punchy headline and the simple graphic while 'diagnostic' polls take longer to construct, conduct and analyse, are more difficult to write up, and usually cost a great deal more to do. Examples of each type have been commissioned from MORI by *The Times*.

The first, taken the day after the Americans bombed Libya, told a story quickly (within 36 hours from a national sample of British adults interviewed in person), fairly cheaply and, as a by-product, gave an interesting test of poll accuracy/reliability.

Early on the morning of Tuesday 15 April 1986 American F-111s flying from British air bases bombed Tripoli and other targets in Libya. Three news media organizations commissioned three different polling companies to test British public opinion: ITN went to Harris Research Centre, the *Daily Telegraph* commissioned Gallup and *The Times* instructed MORI. None of the pollsters knew the others were in the field; all designed their questionnaires independently of each other.

Three different questions on the principal issue were put to three totally independent representative samples of adults across the country. Remarkably similar results were obtained. MORI reported its findings to *The Times* at 3.45 pm on Wednesday, from results obtained from a sample of 1,051 adults interviewed face-to-face by our interviewers in 53 different constituencies from Cunninghame North in Scotland to Truro in Cornwall. At about the same time Harris were reporting to their client, ITN, from 1,029 interviews in 49 sampling points and Gallup's results were being given to the *Daily Telegraph* from their nationally representative quota sample of 1,059 adults interviewed at 44 points across the country. These were the results:

Gallup: *Daily Telegraph*

Do you think the government was right or wrong to allow the Americans to use air bases in Britain for their attack on Libya?

Right	27%
Wrong	69%
Don't know	3%

Harris: ITN

Do you approve or disapprove of the British government's decision to allow American planes based in Britain to take part in the attack on targets in Libya?

Approve	28%
Disapprove	69%
Don't know	4%

MORI: *The Times*

Do you think that Mrs Thatcher was right or wrong to give President Reagan permission for American bombers to fly from British bases to participate in the attack on Libya?

Right	25%
Wrong	71%
No opinion	4%

Those who do not like polls, as well as those who are unknowledgeable about them, say they are not useful because everything depends on how you ask the question, how the sample is drawn and/or who you ask. An independent test such as this, seldom made except at general elections and then only on electoral behaviour and attitudes, shows clearly that attitude measurement on a topical question can be done with confidence when carried out by professional organizations using properly designed, if differing, questions put to properly selected representative samples.

The second type of usage, descriptive/diagnostic research, appeared in *The Times* a few months later, in September 1986, in a series of three news stories, three feature articles and a leader, published over four days, all focusing on a survey of the attitudes of what *The Times* called 'Thatcher's Children', the 18–25-year-old British young adults who have only been of voting age under a Conservative government led by Margaret Thatcher. The survey was a blending of a poll of the attitudes of a representative sample of more than 600 young people, comprising some 19 questions analysed by sex, age, social class, region of the country, voting intention, type of employment, trade union membership etc. (over 300 pages of tabulations), plus six in-depth group discussions in three different parts of England, of a qualitative nature, with a reporter sitting in to witness the trained moderator probing the reasons behind the feelings these young people had. The groups were recorded and extensive verbatim quotations used in the story (with respondents' permission).

Whereas the Libya poll took less than three days from conception to publication and cost of the order of £5,000, the 'Thatcher's Children' effort took over a month and cost well over £15,000. Each in its way made a significant contribution to understanding important public events taking place in Britain at the time. Each combined the skills of the pollster and journalist. Each played its role, one a 'snap' poll, the other more deliberate. Who is to say which is the more reputable, the more newsworthy, the more valuable? The 'Libya' poll was quoted around the world and taken note of in a number of capitals; the 'Thatcher's Children' poll fuelled much thoughtful debate in the political parties in the run-up to Britain's next General Election.

Finally, one wonders how some questions come to be asked.

In 1979, the then editor of the *Daily Express*, Derek Jameson, carried a poll conducted by one Sultan Mamood and 'a team of immigrant researchers' who interviewed in 18 cities (unspecified) some 500 people (unrepresentative), and reported to one decimal point the answer to such questions as: 'Do you intend to remain in Britain forever?'

Qualitative research

In the 'Thatcher's Children' poll referred to above, a blend of statistically sound data from precisely drafted questions asked of a representative sample of a defined universe was buttressed by the illustrative verbatim comments taken from a collection of young people (not chosen to be statistically representative) in six groups, six to eight people in each group, from three marginal Conservative constituencies in three parts of the country. In each group two Conservative, two Labour and two SDP/Liberal Alliance supporters and two 'don't knows' were recruited and quizzed for one-and-a-half to two hours about their feelings and concerns by a trained moderator working from a semi-structured topic guide but allowing the discussion to roam freely around the subject. These groups allowed the journalist to give a flavour to the story that would otherwise have been missing. For a number of years the *Wall Street Journal* has commissioned political pollsters both in The United States and Britain to do such group discussions to gain insight into what key groups of the public are thinking about a given topic at a point in time. Individual depth interviews are sometimes also used to obtain insights into the 'why's' that are behind the 'what's' and 'who's' of sample surveys.

Piloting

It should (but does not) go without saying that new question wording should be tested by trying it out on a few typical respondents to ensure that it means to people what it means to the researcher and the client, that it is clear, unambiguous, understandable, capable of being answered, and unthreatening. Sometimes a sequential piloting is called for, alternately drafting questions, briefing interviewers who each conduct half a dozen pilot interviews, come back and debrief the researchers (who should also do some interviews themselves), who redraft the questions, re-brief the interviewers etc., repeating the cycle until the questions are 'right'.

Evaluating survey interviewing

Journalists pioneered the use of the interview, so they are well aware of its strengths and weaknesses. The typical survey interview, however, is different from the journalistic exchange. The survey interviewer, often working part time from home, works from a set of prepared questions. So it is important to probe into the training and experience of the interviewers when writing about survey results.

Who conducted the survey? Often the reputation of the research firm is all the information one has about the interviewing — the faith that a reputable firm surely has good interviewing. But, it certainly does not hurt to ask a few good questions about the interviewing, even when the firm seems to have a solid reputation. Those questions are best formulated after first evaluating the questionnaire according to the criteria discussed earlier.

In Europe, most experts agree that face-to-face interviewing is still preferable, and all empirical evidence in elections (to my knowledge) in Europe favours personal interviews — as long as they are properly carried out. Regardless of the method of interviewing, however, the most crucial factors in the quality of interviewing are the survey firm's training, control, and careful deployment of interviewers.

Interviewer selection and training

Some survey firms manage their interviewing as an internal function completely under their control. Others sub-contract interviewing to a growing number of professional interviewing firms. Both systems can provide good quality, if proper surveillance is employed.

Interviewer selection becomes especially critical in cases where specific ethnic or social groups are a substantial part of the population studied. Two cases illustrate the problems of race and class bias in interviewing.

> In the early days of the civil rights movement in America two political scientists studied the attitudes and political participation of southern blacks. Because of high racial tension, it was obvious that blacks were required as interviewers to avoid the 'safe', biased answers blacks were likely to provide white interviewers. In recruiting black interviewers, an attempt was made to screen those whose demeanour appeared too middle-class, because many of the respondents were among the rural poor.

> In Great Britain, at a by-election in Brixton, a South London constituency where many voters are black, an exit poll carried out for the BBC found that nearly half of the black voters refused to tell white interviewers how they had cast their votes.

In both cases an attempt was made to minimize the social distance between interviewers and respondents. It is almost impossible to eliminate all differences between interviewers and the sample because of the complexity of most polls. In fact, research suggests some social distance is actually desirable in getting reliable data. The problem, though, is usually how to reduce the social distance rather than the reverse.

Once appropriate interviewers are selected, proper training is required with the actual questionnaire and the method of interviewing being used. Reputable research and interviewing firms conduct training sessions using a pre-tested questionnaire. If telephone interviews from a centralized location are used, monitoring selected interviews helps ensure high quality. But the most crucial factor is the opportunity for interviewer practice using the actual questionnaire.

Strict instructions should be provided for the interviewers about locating respondents. In face-to-face interviewing, respondents are often first selected by housing unit. The person answering the door is briefly interviewed to determine the number of persons living in the household and which person is actually to be interviewed. During a telephone interview the person answering the phone is asked questions to determine household context and who is actually to be interviewed at the sampled number. These search and screening procedures are essential to obtaining a valid sample, so strict training is required at this stage of polling.

One measure of a survey firm's dedication to reliable work is the effort made to obtain interviews with sampled persons who are not at home. At least one call-back, and usually several, is standard procedure for the validity of the survey results in random surveys so they may be generalized to the universe from which they are sampled.

Another indicator of the quality of interviewing is the refusal rate; some interviewers are just more persistent, regularly turning in a more complete assignment, well done, than others.

Validating interviews

One of the most important indicators of quality interviewing is the extent to which interviewers are checked for accuracy and honesty. Interviewers' work may be checked in a variety of ways, some direct and other indirect.

A sample of each interviewer's list of completed interviews may be called on in person or by phone to ask whether they were actually interviewed. In addition, the respondents may be asked to verify that they were asked about all the things covered in the interview schedule so that 'short-cutting' may be detected. Some firms also use a mail follow-up questionnaire to discern respondent attitudes about the effectiveness of the interviewer. Others conduct comparative computer analysis of interviewers' work in order to detect and investigate dramatic differences in the answers received from similar types of persons by separate interviewers.

If telephone interviewing is used, much greater control over possible biases and potential interviewer cheating is possible when a centralized bank of telephones is used at a single location. Much less control is possible if the interviewers are allowed to do telephoning from their own homes.

Interactive interviewing

Interactive microprocessor devices for interviewers as well as for tabulation were introduced to Britain in the early 1980s, but they got little use or attention in this country, unlike some others. Granada Television used such a panel during the 1983 election and to a lesser degree in 1987, but got little notice.[8] Such interactive systems will certainly facilitate getting data from individual interviewers' input through the sets in their own living rooms direct to the central computer. The analyst at his office can then see trends developing, cross-tabbed by demographic, behaviourial and attitudinal characteristics on his set (and protected by the system from snoopers), calling for a print-out whenever wanted for a conference with editor or party leader.

This is the main value of the CATI (Computer Aided Telephone Interviewing) systems employed by several firms to do telephone interviewing. They enable the analyst to dip into the data as it builds up, not having to wait until an interviewer in the field finishes her quota, returns home, adds up and checks her work and phones in the results.

Notes

1 Stanley Payne, *The Art of Asking Questions* (Princeton University Press, 1951).
2 George Gallup, *The Sophisticated Poll Watcher's Guide* (Princeton University Press, 1976).
3 G. Cleveland Wilhoit and David H. Weaver, *Newsroom Guide to Polls and Surveys* (American Newspaper Publishers Association, 1980).
4 Robert M. Worcester and John Downham (eds), *Consumer Market Research Handbook*, 3rd edn (Elsevier North Holland, 1986).
5 Wilhoit and Weaver, *Newsroom Guide*.
6 Robert M. Worcester and Timothy R. Burns, 'A Statistical Examination of the Relative Precision of Verbal Scales', *Journal of the Market Research Society*, 17, no. 3, 1975.
7 Roger J. Stubbs and Peter F. Hutton, 'Yea-saying: Myth or

Reality in Attitude Response?', Paper presented to Market Research Society Conference, 1976.
8 Iain McLean 'Mechanisms for Democracy', in D. Held and C. Pollitt (eds), *New Forms of Democracy* (Sage, 1986).

12 The Science of Sampling

Sir Arthur Conan Doyle, the author of the Sherlock Holmes series, had a view on probability theory:[1]

> While the individual man is an insoluble puzzle, in the aggregate he becomes a mathematical certainty. You can never foretell what any one man will do, but you can say with precision what an average number will be up to. Individuals vary, but averages remain constant.

And Adolphe Quetelet asked 'Must I drink the whole bottle in order to judge the quality of the wine?'[2]

The two questions put to me more often than any others are:

1 'How come I've never been asked? And come to think of it, nobody I know has ever been asked either!' and
2 'How can a sample of only a thousand people possibly be representative of the British public?'

In this section I hope to answer both questions, and many others perhaps less often thought of. To begin, here is what Wilhoit and Weaver[3] have to say on the subject.

> George Gallup effectively uses the spoon of soup analogy to disarm sampling critics. He points out that with the proper stirring, a cook can taste just a spoonful to tell how the entire pot of soup is doing. Sampling is primarily a technical and, in reality, a much simpler problem than question-drafting, interviewing and certainly reporting poll data. It is a bit more complicated than preparing a good pot of soup, but the basic

mechanics and ideas of sampling are easily within the grasp of reporters and editors.

The street-corner survey that has been the basis of thousands of news stories typically uses sampling. It may even be erroneously called a 'random' survey. It is sampling, though, in the sense that a few persons' ideas are assumed to represent an entire community. People commonly use the word 'random' to mean haphazard; the statistician uses it with precision to mean 'having an equal probability of selection'.

What is missing in street-corner samples or straw polls is randomness: the requirement that every person in a community or group being studied has an equal chance of being interviewed. The fact that a person regularly walks past a certain street corner or acts friendly gives that person no greater chance of being interviewed than anyone else in a truly random sample.

Another important factor in survey sampling is to be certain that the precise community, group, or class being talked about in the results is carefully defined. In other words, precisely what is the larger group (commonly called the population or universe) to whose views or attributes the study is generalizing? Is the population referred to in the results actually the one from which the sample is taken?

For example, if an election study attempts to say which candidate is preferred by the electorate of a constituency, then the population from which the sample should be drawn is all registered voters who are likely to vote. Results based upon an analysis of a sample of adults of voting age (unless registered voters are identified and sub-classified) speak to a broader population than the electorate but, in a study for, say, a local authority, this may be appropriate.

By defining the population, the pollster is then able to determine what to use as the sampling frame. The sampling frame is a physical representation of the population, such as a map, listing, or directory from which a sample can actually be drawn. If electors are defined as the population to be studied, then the most accurate sampling frame is the registration records containing the names of those persons registered to vote, even with the knowledge that the register is far from perfect.

Other types of universes might be all Members of Parliament or final-year undergraduates at universities, or residents of York. No sample can ever be representative of any other universe than that from which it is drawn and, practically speaking, no sample (as opposed to a census, that is, asking everybody) is ever perfect.

Sampling methods

Three types of sampling are generally used: random, quota and housing type, which is a form of modified random sampling.

Simple random sampling is the random selection of households, persons, or things from a broadly defined universe, such as adults who are registered to vote. Such a sample, depending upon sample size, may be assumed to be representative of the universe within a certain error margin. Stratified random sampling adds a second technical step to make sure the sample is representative of certain characteristics of the universe. If we know that our universe of adults who are registered to vote can be broken down into categories (or strata) such as young, middle- and older-aged, we may wish to draw simple random samples from each of those groups proportional to each group's size. The end result usually will be a sample with slightly greater sampling error than a simple random sample.

Disproportionate random sampling is similar in approach. Several samples are drawn from different strata of a universe, but these samples are actually disproportionate to the sizes of the strata. The over-sampling of the subgroups enables a pollster to speak with greater assurance about the problems or attitudes of the selected subgroups than would be possible with a simple random sample drawn from the broadly defined population.

For example, if a researcher is interested in comparing attitudes by race towards public schools in a community, roughly equal sample sizes from (say) whites, Asians and blacks would be desirable to give the greatest statistical reliability to the results from each group. A simple random sample from the community, of course, would yield a much smaller number of sampled persons from the minority groups than from the majority group, depending upon their incidence in the universe. What is commonly done is to disproportionately sample each group; for instance, if there were 40% whites and 40% Asians and 20% blacks in the community, one would not draw a random sample of (say) 1,000 as 400 whites, 400 Asians and 200 blacks, as this would give less reliable results for the black sample. Instead, a sample of 334, 333 and 333 would be obtained from the designated 1,000, to give the most reliable comparison, but when reporting the views of the total sample, the 1,000, the results would be 'weighted' in the computer to give the white and Asian 334/333 the 'weight' of 400 each and reduce the 'weight' of the 333 blacks to 200, the 'proper' or 'representative' proportion they constitute in the community from which the sample is drawn (see below).

Quota samples are the more frequently used, and empirically have the greater accuracy record in Britain. Quotas are set for each unit, such as constituency, by reference to census data for such characteristics as age, sex, social class and work or housing status and the interviewer directed to fill his or her quota with electors whose characteristics fulfil the quota given.

Housing-based samples are now frequently used, especially for local constituency surveys, regionally based samples and the like, using a classification of types of housing and occupants. This combines the random and quota methods and provides accurate samples. Other modified sampling includes random walk designs, taking every (say) fifth house from a designated starting place, random digit dialling in telephone polls rather than a random selection from telephone books to ensure that ex-directory numbers are caught, etc.

Weighting techniques

Whatever form of sampling is used, the proportion of persons in a sample from a subgroup of a larger population may sometimes be more or less than the actual proportion of that subgroup in the larger population, either by design, as above, or by accident. A way of dealing with the problem is to weight the subgroup results differently from other parts of the sample.

For example, suppose we draw a simple random sample of a community and find that the proportion of middle-class persons sampled is only half of the group's actual size in the community (based on census data). The results of question answers from middle-class persons in our sample may be doubled, so that an overall estimate of community opinion based on the survey will reflect (represent) the community more precisely. This weighting is especially necessary in correcting random samples, in which, even after four or five call-backs to attempt to ensure that as high a response rate as possible is obtained, working men and women and young people, more likely to be out to the cinema or pub, will be under-represented and old age pensioners, the less gregarious and the television addicts are more likely to be found at home.

It is not often that simple 'drawing names out of a hat' randomness is feasible in sampling. Because of mechanical and economic difficulties, modifications to random sampling are often made. These modifications usually incorporate some form of geographic selection, systemization, and/or clustering.

In the first stage for a national face-to-face study, the country is divided into primary geographic areas. These primary areas are typically metropolitan areas or small groups of counties in the United States, the parliamentary constituency in Great Britain and housing registers in The Netherlands, where there is no central registration system. From these primary areas, units are selected randomly.

Stage two involves sampling locations within the primary unit. The primary unit is divided into strata of cities, towns and rural areas in the United States, constituencies are divided into wards in Britain. In a typical unit we may have one very large city, several towns and the surrounding country area. The large city (if only one), one of the towns (chosen randomly), and the remaining rural area become the sampling locations in the United States, (say) four out of the sixteen wards in the parliamentary constituency in Britain.

In stage three, the sampling locations are then divided into smaller bits, usually identifiable areas such as city blocks or townships or enumeration districts. Next, some of these bits are chosen randomly (stage four). The chunks are divided into segments (clusters) of about 20 (or fewer) housing units, from which a systematic random sample of housing units is selected.

This process typically is designed to yield a sample of persons from 1,000 to 2,000 in size. The interviewer is the person who is actually responsible for getting the right persons in the households to respond, based upon the number, sex and ages of the persons living in each dwelling. It is at this point that randomness can be lost if the interviewer does not follow precisely the directions for respondent selection. So, the motivation, honesty and training of interviewers again becomes a crucial criterion for a valid survey.

Telephone sampling

Interviewing by telephone is increasing in most countries. Telephone samples typically are easy to construct from directories, but they must contend with the bias of both non-subscribers and unlisted numbers. Estimates of unlisted numbers range from as high as 40% in major cities in the United States to less than 5% in rural areas in Britain. To contend with the problem, pollsters use a combination of systematic random sampling from published directories and a random digit modification.

After establishing a systematic random selection of telephone numbers from a phone directory, business numbers are eliminated. The last one, two or three digits of the chosen telephone numbers are substituted with random digits taken from a random numbers table. This combination of procedures includes unlisted numbers in the sample and decreases the chances of reaching a business or institutional phone.

When presented with data collected from a telephone survey, good questions to ask in assessing the survey's reliability are:

- What steps were taken to deal with unlisted telephones?
- What is the bias inherent in leaving people who are not on the telephone out of the sample?
- How was the effect of this bias dealt with?
- What was the refusal rate, by subgroup of the sample?
- How was unbalanced refusal by various subgroups dealt with?
- Were the questions suitable for asking over the telephone?
- What is the record of the pollster in getting it right?
- How many questions were asked?
- What techniques were used to get around the inability to use show cards, illustrations or other visual prompts?

Sampling size and confidence intervals

Survey sample size is often the key to evaluating whether the conclusions a pollster draws from a study are warranted, once it has been established that some form of probability sampling was used. One of the key questions to ask is: 'What is the estimated sampling error tolerance?'

Sampling error is an estimate of the range of possible error in the survey results attributable to random sampling alone. Other error of a human and mechanical nature may also be present, as is implied in the earlier discussion of questions and interviewing techniques.

Three major factors are involved in estimating sampling error tolerance: the size of the actual sample, the probability level (or level or confidence) used with the data analysis, and the estimate of how heterogeneous, or diverse, the universe under study is on the major factors being asked about in the survey.

Probability level may be thought of as the betting odds that any particular sample survey result is within the sampling error estimate. In other words, are we 50%, 67%, 95% or 99% sure that the sample data represent the universe from which the sample was drawn within a specified tolerance?

Universe heterogeneity is simply an estimate of the extent of likely variation in a particular community on the topics asked about in the study. In other words, if census data indicate that most people in a community are elderly, then the universe heterogeneity on age would be estimated to be rather low.

In general, holding one of the factors constant, we may assume these things:

- The larger the sample size, the smaller the estimated sampling error. (See Table 12.1 for illustrations of this point.)
- The greater the betting odds (going from 50% certainty to 99% certainty, for example), the greater the sampling error.
- The greater the degree of heterogeneity in a sampled universe, the greater the estimated sampling error.
- The greater the number of sampling points, the smaller the potential sampling error, and interviewer bias error, and heterogeneity error as well.

As a conservative measure, it is a frequent practice to assume the maximum possible universe heterogeneity (that is, a 50%/50% split) in estimating sampling error. Table 12.1 on sampling tolerance makes this assumption and thus contains the largest possible sampling error for each random sample size.

Let us take a practical example to illustrate the use of the table. Imagine that 70% of a random subsample of 200 men and 50% of a random subsample of 250 women (from the same survey totalling a sample of 450 persons) say they are in favour of a particular political party. Remember that the percentage difference between the men and women on political choice must be greater than the sum of the sampling error for men (based on a sample size of 200) and the sampling error for women (based on a sample size of 250).

Consult Table 12.1. At the 95% level of confidence (column 2, the most frequently used level), the sampling tolerance estimate for the 200 sampled men is 6.9 percentage points. The sampling tolerance estimate for the 250 sampled women is 6.2 percentage points. The 95% confidence interval of the difference between these figures is greater than either of the individual intervals, but less than their sum. This can form the basis of a useful 'quick check', since if the actual difference exceeds the sum, then it is certainly 'significant'. In this example it is, since 20 percentage points exceeds (6.9 + 6.2 =) 13.1 percentage points. (If it does not, a more exact test may have to be used — the square root of the sum of the squared individual confidence intervals — and an expert consulted!)

The important things to understand about these factors are these:

(1) The size of the universe. In most cases, the size of the universe being studied has very little to do with the estimate of confidence intervals. A sample of 2,000 persons is just as reliable in a country the size of Ireland (2.5 million adults), The Netherlands or Denmark (3–5 million adults) as in France, Germany or Great Britain (c. 40 million adults) or even the United States (c. 160 million adults). This is one of the hardest facts for people to swallow, whether it be in first-year statistics or from television interviews on election night.

(2) The probability level or level of confidence. Usually, poll results are reported at the 95% probability level. If a poll report is dealing with a particularly crucial election (or an extremely controversial, important community issue) the reporter writing up the survey results might ask: 'What is the estimate of confidence intervals at the 99% probability level for this particular question?'

This might make a difference in a story written about the subject, because a survey that shows a margin of preference for a certain candidate (at the 95% level) may be too close to call at the 99% level. For example (see Table 12.1), a sample size of 350 persons has an estimated confidence interval of about plus or minus 5 percentage points at the 95% level. At the 99% level, the interval is about plus or minus 7 percentage points.

The size of confidence intervals varies not only with the probability level, but with sample size. It is a square-root relationship, so that to halve the confidence interval, a sample size four times as large is required.

Table 12.1 Confidence intervals for random samples of various sizes

Sample size	Tolerance at the 95% Probability	Tolerance at the 99% Probability
	%	%
10	30.1	40.1
25	19.6	25.8
50	13.9	18.2
100	9.8	12.9
150	8.0	10.6
200	6.9	9.1
250	6.2	8.2
300	5.7	7.5
350	5.2	6.9
400	4.9	6.5
450	4.6	6.1
500	4.4	5.8
600	4.0	5.3
700	3.7	4.9
800	3.5	4.6
900	3.3	4.3
1,000	3.1	4.1
1,200	2.8	3.7
1,500	2.5	3.3
2,000	2.2	2.9
2,500	2.0	2.6
3,000	1.8	2.4
5,000	1.4	1.8
10,000	1.0	1.3
25,000	0.6	0.8
50,000	0.4	0.6

It is also true to say that reports of polls should not go overboard on sampling error. It is common in the United States for polls to be tagged with the statement that 'there is a ±3% margin of error on the survey results' as if everything over a 3% difference is important and everything under is not. In fact, if in a battery of mixed positive and negative image attributes a consistent small shift in the same direction is measured, yet some are individually significant, it may well be said that an important shift has been measured.

Finally, remember that it is not true to say, as is often forgotten, that because 19 out of 20 polls will be accurate to ±3% that one in 20 will not be. It may be accurate, but more likely will not be.

(3)   The diversity of the universe or population under study. Just as important as the overall sampling tolerance estimate is whether the sample is large enough to enable comparisons of subsets of the sample, such as old compared to young, urban to rural, or informed to uninformed. The sampling tolerance reported in most surveys is for the overall sample and not for the subsets. A good rule of thumb is that subsets of 100 have to differ by more than about 14 percentage points to be reported as true differences. In questioning a polls results, do not hesitate to ask: 'Are the differences in the subgroups based upon sample sizes sufficient to conclude they are true differences?'

Non-response error

Sampling error is just one source of error in a poll. Another, and potentially more serious, source of error is non-response bias. Non-response bias is that resulting from persons in the sample who either refused to be interviewed or who were not located. The key question is: 'What is the proportion of non-response in the sample, and is there evidence that any particular subgroup of persons was more likely not to respond?' Over the years, non-response typically has been greater in telephone surveys than in face-to-face interviews.

Two situations call for particularly close scrutiny of telephone samples. If the study concerns low-income persons, they are likely to have a low incidence of telephone access, thus a telephone sample of those persons may be inadequate. Secondly, if the questionnaire makes strong reliance upon household income estimates, the telephone method may not produce reliable data because of non-response to particular questions in the survey.

One quick way to get at the possible effects of non-response and to evaluate the overall sample is to look at how the demographic results in the study reflect population statistics available from the government census. For example, if the survey results closely reflect the proportions of urban−rural, men−women, and varying educational and income levels, then one has greater confidence that the sample is representative of other more important factors at issue.

Quota samples

With the aid of official (usually census) data regarding the population, details of a sample to be interviewed in a specific area are established. These details may include age, sex, income category, type of housing, etc. Interviewers are asked to visit and interview in specific areas people with the specified combination of characteristics. Differences can then be corrected by weighting (see above).

Increasingly, pollsters are using quota sampling methods in face-to-face interviewing. One reason for this is the time it takes to call back and back and back on specified respondents drawn, say, from electoral rolls. Another reason is that electoral rolls are increasingly inaccurate in many countries and introduce a systematic bias working against younger, poorer and minority group people.

A third reason is cost; it is usually somewhat cheaper to conduct surveys by use of quota samples. Finally, empirically it has been shown in several countries that properly conducted and controlled quota samples are as good as − or even better than − imperfect (as they must be) random samples of similar size.

Volumes have been written about the advantages and disadvantages of the two systems. Suffice it to say that a reasonable sample can be formed with both systems, provided that the instructions are strictly adhered to. However, in both cases − even if all the people could be interviewed − the sample obtained is not 'ideal'. The result is therefore that the accuracy margins are sometimes wider than Table 12.1 produces, but frequently are even better. The values in Table 12.1 are reasonably satisfactory for a rough estimation of the margins. It is well to keep this in mind when interpreting a survey.

In either case, random or quota, an important rule must be borne in mind, that is, doubling the sample size increases its statistical reliability by only half. A sample of 1,000 is not twice as good as one of 500, only half as good again; a sample of 2,000 is not twice as good as one of 1,000 − but it is, exactly, twice as good as one of 500. Why, you may then ask, go to a larger sample? The answer is usually to increase the statistical accuracy of its sub-samples, so you can look with reasonable accuracy at the Liberal Democratic Party supporters in the sample; or young people, or trade union members.

Panel studies

Another question sometimes asked of pollsters is 'Do you always go to the same people?' and the answer is: 'Not usually, no.' Some organizations doing market research will interview certain consumers about their attitudes to a product category, then persuade them to take samples of a new product for trial for a week or two and then return to interview them again. This technique is called 'placement and call-back'. It is a form of 'panel' study.

Another use of panels, that is asking the same people over and over again, is for measuring behaviour, for example, watching television, buying petrol. The method is sometimes also used in election polling, as it allows researchers and their clients, usually political parties, to measure what is happening to each individual's attitudes and behavioural as opposed to what is happening in the aggregate. For instance, if between two surveys the Conservatives have gained 2 and Labour has lost 2%, it may be that 14 people in 100 have moved one way and 16 another, or just four and two. Panels pinpoint this; thay also enable researchers to probe why things have happened: 'Last week you said you were in favour of the Prime Minister's actions ... now you say you are opposed: what has caused you to change your mind?' There is considerable evidence to show that many people are incapable of remembering what they thought, or in some cases, did previously. Such recall measures as past voting behaviour are notoriously unreliable.

The chief limitation of panel studies is recruitment of people willing to take part. Some people initially willing to be interviewed, get fed up after being interviewed on the same subject for the nth time. Problems such as 'decay' (losing respondents due to drop-out), 'top-up' (replacing drop-outs), panel bias (paying closer attention to the election propaganda in anticipation of being asked about it and thus becoming unrepresentative) and problems of analysis are also associated with panel surveys. Panels also become very difficult to analyse as people drop in and out of them.

Special samples

Other kinds of samples include those of special sections of the public, for example parliamentarians, the elderly, people in a certain area etc. One special kind of survey, offered in every developed and many under-developed countries, is the omnibus survey. Every week, fortnight, month, or whenever, a research organization will undertake a survey of 1,000 or 1,500 or 2,000 adults nationwide, collecting demographic and some attitudinal (e.g. voting intention) data and offering customers the opportunity to 'hitch-hike' or 'piggy-back' questions on to the survey. Usually these surveys take a few weeks to process, but they can provide, say, an editor with an inexpensive means by which data can be obtained to give a statistical base to a story. One example of this was a newspaper which used an omnibus survey to find out how many people had either participated in, went out to see, or viewed on television, a variety of sporting events to include in a feature about sports.

Polling methodology

Polling techniques have evolved in Britain to the point that polls commissioned one evening can be conducted nationally the next day with representative samples of over 1,000 respondents using tightly interlocking quota controls in face-to-face personal interview of some dozen or so questions and reported back the same afternoon.

The 1979 General Election saw the first use of telephone surveys in election polls in Britain, by Marplan. As the telephone penetration in Britain was then only 60%, many were sceptical of their value, especially for voting intention measurement and their record in the 1979 and 1983 elections was not good. In the 1987 General Election, however, with telephone incidence nearly 85% and with much careful study made of weighting procedures and application made to correct the bias, a good result was obtained, as reported earlier. An unpublished analysis by NOP,[4] comparing the voting intention of respondents with telephones with those without, indicated a Tory bias of between 11% and 13%; normal weighting procedures using an 84-cell interlocking matrix of sex, age, social class and region reduced this bias to about 6%, but never could really effectively control for it. This bias makes many attitudinal measures suspect to some degree as well. As telephone ownership continues to increase, such bias will gradually diminish.

As indicated above, turnout measures are sometimes helpful, sometimes not. Normally, Conservatives are more likely to have a higher propensity to vote, but in the winter election of 1974 Labour supporters were more keen to get the Conservatives out than the Tories were to keep Mr Heath in office.

Conventional wisdom holds that since Labour voters are less committed to go to the polls than Conservatives, they will be more likely to stay home when it rains. Also, most observers generally assume that overall turnout will fall if the weather is bad. Neither of these assumptions held true in either 1974 election, so adjustments in forecast polls to take these factors into account would have worsened the error in 1974. In 1979, however, the Tory lead was indeed greater in the 15% of the country that had rain, by a substantial factor.

The examination of panel data, where respondents have been interviewed repeatedly, has shown a biasing effect, but mainly one of increasing interest in the outcome and thereby increasing turnout.

As mentioned above, most pollsters in Britain have now turned from random to quota sampling. Empirical evidence has shown that by itself random sampling has not improved election forecasts. There are a number of hypotheses for this, despite the fact that the mandatory voter resignation system has given British researchers an excellent, annually updated, sampling frame. Each autumn a voter registration form is delivered to every household in the country. If the form is not filled in and returned smartly, a none-too-gentle reminder subsequently arrives through the letter box stating that the fine for not registering is £50. Even then, the register is never completely accurate. Deaths occur between completion of the forms in mid-October and publication of the registers in mid-February. There is emigration overseas. There is some legitimate duplication. There are many movers who, for the most part, cannot economically be followed by the pollster (although most have a postal vote, another source of error), and there is, inevitably, human error in the electoral roll compilation. It was estimated by Butler and O'Muircheartaigh[5] that in mid year — say June — the register is only 92.5% effective. Office of Population Censuses and Surveys researchers Jean Todd and Bob Butcher[6] conducted a thorough study comparing the 1981 Census and a large-scale sample, 14,013 people, living in private households in Great Britain, to determine the efficacy of the electoral roll. They found:

- 6.5% of eligible people were left off the register;
- between 6% and 9% of the names on the register were for people who were not eligible and should not have been listed;
- at best, when the register is new, it is about 9% inaccurate because of movement, and this increases to about 16% at the end of the register's one-year lifetime, i.e., by mid February the following year;
- about a quarter (24%) of eligible 17-year-olds are not registered;
- New Commonwealth citizens have a particularly high non-registration rate of 31%.

Recent years have seen a substantial increase in the number of working women, making electoral register contacts that much more difficult during the day; people generally and the young especially are less easy to contact; and studies have shown that refusal rates, although still not a big factor, have risen in recent years. The repeated recalls required for respectably high completion rates on random surveys cost time and money. In the heat of a General Election both are at a premium. The ability to poll late carries with it a significant advantage, and the interlocking quota controls (frequently sex by age by social class with an override on working women and retired people), while increasing cost often to the same level as random surveys, can be done quicker. That factor (and the relative failure of random samples in recent years to prove to be more accurate) has led to the now nearly universal use of quota samples. And it is worth mentioning that there appears to be some evidence that the introduction of the Community Change in having some effect on Electoral Registration.

Finally, how come *you* have never been asked? Normally polls are conducted in a set of specified constituencies, so if you do not live in one of those, we will not be asking you your opinion. If you do, we would on average expect to interview you once every hundred years or so. If we have not got there yet, hold on, we're coming.

Notes

1 George Gallup, *The Sophisticated Poll Watcher's Guide* (Princeton University Press, 1976).
2 Ibid.
3 G. Cleveland Wilhoit and David H. Weaver, *Newsroom Guide to Polls and Surveys* (American Newspaper Publishers Association, 1980).
4 John O'Brien, 'Telephone Interviewing', unpublished paper, NOP, May 1980.
5 David Butler and Colm O'Muircheartaigh, 'What is 40%?: A note on the eligible electorate', unpublished paper dated 13 February 1979.
6 J. Todd and B. Butcher, *Electoral Registration in 1981*, OPCS, 1982.

13 Adding Up the Figures

The computer is programmed to analyse the data from the survey in whatever way is specified by the researcher. In most surveys the analysis will include, as well as the 'total' or 'top-line' results for the sample as a whole, the results of the 'sub-groups' within the sample, such as for men and women, by age, social class, etc. It is in the details of attitudinal analysis by sub-group that some of the most newsworthy material may be found. Yet most journalists, when confronted by a mound of printout, will recoil in horror. The more delving among them will take the time (some) and trouble (not much) to learn their way around a set of tabulations and will be rewarded by their efforts with a more insightful story, feature or leader that will reflect the subtleties of public opinion in addition to its blunt edge.

As well as demographic (sex, age, class) and regional (area) analysis, the media — at least in Britain — have recently discovered attitudinal, or psychographic, analysis, such as that done for the Labour party by MORI in 1974 (see ch. 4 above). This is one form of a computer-aided technique or group of techniques called multivariate analyses. The most basic attitudinal analysis is the grouping of people by their voting intentions. More complicated, but decades old, is the grouping or segmenting of people by their personality characteristics, beliefs or feelings that link certain clusters of people who are indistinguishable by demographics but are none the less groupable and identifiable by their attitudes, such as in market research for airlines – 'fear-flyers' and 'fun-flyers' – or for banks – 'spenders' and 'savers'. Few journalists have discovered and made good use of these groupings, yet some of the most advanced use of psychographics has been in the marketing departments of newspapers.[1]

Handling percentages

Both percentiles and percentages are useful for describing how different things are related to each other on a scale of 1 to 100. For example, if you know that someone's score on time spent with newspapers is in the 80th percentile, then you also know that nearly four-fifths of the other scores (79%) fall below this person's score and one-fifth of the scores (20%) fall above it. Whereas percentiles refer to individual scores or measures of some kind, percentages refer to groups of scores, measures, responses or whatever. And because survey answers are usually sorted into groups, percentages are more common in survey research than percentiles.

Calculating percentages is easy once you determine what the base (or total number) is. For example, if 500 persons are included in a survey and 250 of them respond in a certain way, you calculate the percentage of all persons in the survey responding in that way by dividing the number who respond that way (250) by the base (500) and multiplying by $100\% = 250/500 \times 100 = 50\%$. In looking at percentages in survey research the question to keep asking is: 'What is the base of this percentage?' Upon what is this percentage based? All persons included in the survey? Only registered voters? Only women?

One common error is using percentages when the bases are too small. If 15 persons answer that they intend to vote for Candidate X in the upcoming election, and five persons say they intend to vote for Candidate Y (with all others in the survey answering that they are undecided), it is misleading to tell the reader that 75% of the decided voters are for Candidate X, versus only 25% for Candidate Y. It is far better to point out that of the 100 persons surveyed, only 20 were decided, and of the 20 decided, 15 were for X and five for Y.

In other words, when the base is small (less than 80 cases or so), use the actual numbers rather than converting them to percentages. In any case, it is usually misleading to re-calculate percentages to leave out the 'don't knows' to attitudinal questions – on the other hand it is usually equally misleading to fail to re-percentage voting intention questions, as they are used to compare to the previous election's result. Newspaper reports on the polls in the run-up to the 1990 East German election were for the most part misleading, seemingly either reporting huge levels of 'don't knows', over 50% in some cases, and reporting 'SPD leads by 8' when reporting a 15% to 7% share, having failed to reallocate the 'don't knows' or, reallocating the 'don't knows' but comparing the adjusted results to other papers' reports which did not.

It is important to remember too that percentages calculated with different bases cannot be directly compared to each other without some explanation as to what their bases are. That is, you cannot accurately say that 50% of the persons in the survey answered a question a certain way compared to 40% who answered another question a certain way unless the base is the same for both percentages. If the base is not the same, journalists should in their write-up specify it along with the percentage. For example, the report should say that 50% of all persons included in the survey answered a question in a certain way, compared to 40% of registered electors who answered the same question in that way.

It is usually useful to convert numbers of responses to percentages so as to be able to talk about the proportions of people answering one way or another, and to be able to compare the patterns of answers from one survey to another, unless the numbers on which the percentages are based are small. In dealing with polls and surveys, the reader should keep in mind the difference between percentages and percentage points. This is especially true when calculating sampling error tolerances.

For example, the sampling tolerances given in Table 12.1 (p. 160) are percentage points, not percentages. In looking at this table, you can see that for a random sample of 400 persons at the 95% confidence level, the error tolerance is plus or minus 4.9 percentage points. This means that you add and subtract 4.9 to whatever the percentage is for the sample — say, 40% — to get the estimate for the population from which the sample was drawn (35.1% to 44.9% in this case). You do not take 4.9% of 40% (1.96) and add and subtract it to get the estimate for the population because the 4.9 represents percentage points, rather than a percentage.

Occasionally in analysing survey data it becomes necessary to calculate percentages over time to determine how much gain or loss has occurred. Usually the earliest time period becomes the base. For example, if a survey of newspaper readers in 1989 indicated that they spend about 30 minutes with the newspaper each day, and another such survey in 1990 indicates that they spend about 35 minutes a day, what is the percentage gain? Usually this is calculated by dividing the change (plus 5 minutes) by the earlier (1989) figure of 30 minutes and multiplying by 100% change = 5/30 × 100 = 16.7%. This calculation tells us that from 1989 to 1990, there was a 16.7% increase in the number of minutes spent with the newspaper. Whenever you encounter percentages of gain or loss, you should check to make sure that the base is the earlier figure.

In looking at differences in percentages in survey data, the primary question to keep asking is: 'Are these differences greater than plus or minus the sampling error tolerance for the survey?' (Table 12.1 gives sampling error tolerances for random samples of various sizes.) It is fairly common for those who report surveys to interpret even small differences in percentages as meaningful when such differences could be due entirely to sampling tolerances. For example, in a survey of 1,000 properly selected persons with a reasonably high response rate (80% or more), the sampling tolerance is plus or minus 3 percentage points or so. This means, say, that differences in lead between the parties' percentages should be 6 percentage points or greater to be interpreted as meaningful, because both adding and subtracting 3 percentage points from each percentage produces a range of 6 percentage points. Yet the lead figure is the one most often reported, especially in headlines, and changes or shifts in lead are subject to the greatest margin of error. When the figures are 'on the margin', it is time to take especial care — and consult the experts.

In my very early days working for the Labour party, the then Leader of the Opposition, Harold Wilson, was serving as President of the Royal Statistical Society. Things were pretty grim for him, but a private poll result which had been reported by me to his entourage showed a 2% increase in the Labour share of the poll. Encouraging, but *not* statistically significant, according to anyone's calculations. Yet in a lunchtime speech at which members of the press were present Mr Wilson mentioned the 'significant' news he had been given, that Labour was coming back in the private figures I had given the party. I read about this in the afternoon paper, and immediately protested, saying that the majority of MPs might be forgiven for describing a two point rise as significant (and not revealing what the figures were), but not the President of the Royal Statistical Society. Told that evening of my protest, Harold Wilson sent his apology and promised not to repeat the offence — and he never did.

The same rules apply to checking percentages in tables as apply to checking them in the text of a report, but there are a few new twists. One should still keep asking if the differences in percentages are greater than two times the sampling error tolerance, but another problem with interpreting percentages in tables is deciding how to compute them. Should the percentages be based on the totals for each row or the totals for each column of the table?

When comparing different groups to each other, the percentages should always be calculated on the totals for each group. Because various groups of people in surveys are rarely equal in size, it is usually necessary to compare the percentages based on the totals for each group, rather than the raw numbers.

Often journalists and survey researchers will collapse several answer categories into one to make the presentation of the data simpler or to increase the number of responses in each category. There is nothing inherently wrong with this practice, as long as the journalist and the reader understand what the actual responses were and how they were added together to form new categories. For example, in asking about how the public rates US presidents, Gallup gives his respondents two choices — 'approve or disapprove'. But Harris gives his respondents four choices — 'excellent, pretty good, only fair, or poor'. Harris's four choices are often collapsed into two — 'positive' (excellent and pretty good) and 'negative' (only fair and poor). In the past few years, Gallup's average 'approval' rating has tended to be somewhat higher than Harris's 'positive' ratings. Although there is nothing basically wrong with this discrepancy, the readers should understand how each pollster arrives at his ratings.

In a table reporting Harris's findings, for example, the journalist should make sure that after the 'positive' category the words 'excellent' and 'pretty good' appear, a follows:

How do you rate the job President Reagan is doing as President?

Positive ('excellent' and 'pretty good')	46%	
Negative ('only fair' and 'poor')	52%	
Undecided/no answer	2%	
TOTAL	100%	(1,504 — or whatever the total number of respondents is)

Another example of collapsing answer categories occurs in the Gallup and Harris questions on the amount of confidence people have in various American institutions. Harris gives his respondents three choices — 'a great deal, only some, and hardly any'. Gallup gives his respondents five choices — 'a great deal, quite a lot, some, very little, and none'. When these answer categories are collapsed into 'positive' and 'negative' responses, it is not surprising that Gallup finds much more confidence in various American institutions than does Harris, because Gallup offers two 'positive' responses ('a great deal' and 'quite a lot'), whereas Harris offers only one 'positive' response ('a great deal').

Again, the point is not that Gallup is right and Harris wrong, but only that in comparing 'positive' responses from each poll, the journalist and the reader should understand the choices given a respondent that make up a 'positive' response. And the same is true for 'negative' responses, or for any other survey responses which are based on a combination of more than one answer category.

Calculating averages

Averages are often used in survey research (and in other kinds of research) to summarize measures taken from a group of things (persons, documents etc.). Although averages can be very useful summaries, they can also be ambiguous and misleading, depending on the nature of the groups they are supposed to represent and the kind of average used. In general, the more diverse the group, the less meaningful averages are. The key concept is that averages should be representative of the group.

The most commonly used average is the **mean**, which is calculated by adding all the answers (or measures) and dividing by the number of things (persons, documents etc.) in the group. For example, if 25 families are represented in a survey and they have the following incomes the mean is found by calculating the total income and dividing by the total number of families.

No. of families		Annual income	
1	×	£150,000 =	£150,000
1	×	50,000 =	50,000
2	×	30,000 =	60,000
4	×	15,000 =	60,000
6	×	10,000 =	60,000
11	×	6,000 =	66,000
		TOTAL	£446,000

When all 25 incomes are added together and divided by 25, we find that the mean income for this group of families is £17,840. But when we look at the actual incomes of these 25 families, we find that only four families are making more than £15,000 a year, so the mean of £17,840 is an inflated average and tends to be misleading. Why is this so?

The mean is sensitive to extremely high or extremely low income values. In this case, we have one family with an extremely high income (£150,000) and three families with noticeably higher incomes than the other families (£50,000 and £30,000). These unusually high incomes tend to pull the mean upward, or artificially to inflate it. Therefore, when using the mean as an average, be sure to check on whether there are any unusually high or low values. If so, look (or ask the researcher if you are in a position to do so) for other average measures, such as the median or the mode.

The **median** is simply the midpoint value − that is, the middle value above which one-half of the cases lie and below which one-half of the cases lie. In the example of the 25 families used here, the median family income is somewhere between £15,000 and £10,000 because if we count down from the top, the imaginary 'middle family' (which falls between the 12th and 13th family) makes less than £15,000 a year but more than £10,000 a year. As it turns out, by a process known as 'interpolation' we can estimate the median to be £10,400.

As can be seen, the estimated median of £10,400 is a more accurate estimate of the 'average' income of these 25 families than is the mean of £17,840. The median is thus generally a better average measure than the more commonly used mean when there are a few extremely high or a few extremely low values.

A third kind of average is the **mode** − the most frequent value or response. In the sample of the 25 family incomes, the modal income is clearly £6,000 because 11 of the 25 families have this income. The next most frequent income is £10,000, with six families. But if we used the mode to represent the 'average' income of these 25 families, we would be underestimating annual family income because 14 of the 25 families have considerably higher annual incomes than £6,000. The mode is often not a good average measure because it can occur anywhere − at the top, middle or bottom of the scale.

Given the differences between the mean, the median and the mode, how do you decide which is a more accurate summary of the average? Begin by comparing the three values. If they are similar in value, use the mean because it is the most common measure of the average and the one most people are most likely to understand. But if the mean and the median differ considerably, it is best to use the median as the measure of the average. If the mode differs considerably from the median and the mean (as it does in the example of 25 family incomes used in the previous section), it would be helpful to know both the median and the mode if possible.

Remember that the closer the individual scores are to each other (be they annual incomes, minutes per day spent with a newspaper, or whatever), the better the average represents all the individual measures. It is useful to report on the lowest and highest measures and to give some idea of how close the measures are to each other.

Going back to the example of the 25 families, a journalist could summarize the data on their annual incomes by writing:

Although their incomes ranged from a low of £6,000 to a high of £150,000, the middle income of these 25 families was £10,400. But the most common income was £6,000, the amount reported by 11 of the 25 families.

Note that in this description the mean of £17,840 is not even mentioned because it is so much higher than the median of £10,400 and the mode of £6,000. Of course, this example was designed to illustrate differences between the mean, median and mode. In real-world situations, these differences may not be so pronounced.

Swing

A useful concept used in Britain to explain changes in voting intention or the public's position on issues is the measure of 'swing'. More often used than understood, it is based on the idea that the difference in share of voting intention between two points in time can be described in a single number, and it can be used, although less effectively, in a multiple party or issue situation. It is most effective in a two-party situation, e.g. United States, although it is rarely used in America. Swing is calculated by subtracting the difference between two sets of figures and dividing by two, simple as that.

GENERAL ELECTION SHARE OF VOTE

	1979 %	1983 %	Difference %
Con	45	44	−1
Lab	38	28	−10
Lib/SDP	14	26	+12
Other	3	2	−1
Con lead	+7	+16	+9
Swing			+4.5

The net difference between the Conservative and Labour change between the two elections is +9 (−1(−)−10), which divided by two equals +4.5. Thus a journalist would write that 'There was a four and a half per cent "swing" from Labour to the Conservatives as a result of the Alliance increasing their "share" from 14% to 26%.'

A simple example would be in comparing the EEC referendum with a poll taken after the 1974 General Election six months previously.

	Opinion poll %	Referendum %	Difference %
'In'	45	67	+22
'Out'	55	33	−22
'In' lead	−10	+34	+44
Swing			+22

So a ten point 'out' poll became a 33 point 'in' vote when the referendum came, which was the result of a 22% 'swing' in the electorate, among those who voted/expressed a voting intention.

It is for this reason that the custom in Great Britain is to reallocate the 'don't knows' (will not votes/undecideds/refused) when reporting voting intention, although it is good practice to report those who express no opinion as a percentage of the total, e.g. 'The "outs" had a ten point lead over the "ins", after reallocating 15% who said they did not intend to vote, were undecided or refused to express a view.'

Reallocation of voting intention figures

Reallocation is done by repercentaging the share figures for each party on the base of those expressing voting intention, e.g. dividing 32% by 83%, 30% by 83%, 20% by 83% and 1% by 83%, as in the example below:

How would you vote if there were a general election tomorrow?

	Poll %	Reallocated %
Con	32	39
Lab	30	36
Lib/SDP	20	24
Other	1	1
Sub-total	83	100
Would not vote	10	10
Undecided	6	6
Refused	1	1
'Don't knows'		17

This reallocation should in my view always be done when comparing voting intention to actual voting results and never be done at any other time. Using the example above, to compare the unallocated poll results to the 1983 General Election share is nonsense, as:

	1983 results %	Poll results %	Change of share %
Con	44	32	−12
Lab	28	30	+2
Lib/SDP	26	20	−6
Other	2	1	−1
Con lead	−16	+2	+14
Swing			+7%

Whereas it makes sense when reallocated:

	1983 results %	Poll results %	Change of share %
Con	44	39	−5
Lab	28	36	+8
Lib/SDP	26	24	−2
Other	2	1	−1
Con lead	+16	+3	+13
Swing			+6.5%

Notes

1 G. Cleveland Wilhoit and David H. Weaver make some excellent, basic points about the 'numbers' side of polls in their *Newsroom Guide to Polls and Surveys* (American Newspaper Publishers Association, 1980).

14 Publishing Survey Results: the Bottom Line

Four out of five adults in Britain read at least one national newspaper daily, and many read more than one. Throughout the towns and villages of Britain are local newsagents, many of whom employ newsboys and girls to deliver the morning paper well before breakfast. There are some ten or a dozen national dailies to choose from, running the political, social and economic spectrum of opinion and taste, and another three or four in Scotland. On Sundays, there are now five 'qualities' where there were three a year or two ago, and all now run to several sections, magazines and inserts. The market is highly competitive and financial pressures are significant (several run at losses of substantial magnitude).

Opinion polls are an expensive form of journalism, yet nearly every national and Scottish newspaper sponsors its own poll at election times (and most between elections as well). All newspapers report all the others' polls, sometimes at considerable length, as do the television news programmes. Yet a love–hate relationship exists between the polls and the press.

This relationship is based on the need of newspapers for something better than what one editor once described to me as 'sniffing the London air'. Polls provide instant expertise, polls make news, and polls provide a natural whipping boy if something goes wrong, as it did in 1970 and again in February 1974. Ivor Crewe[1] propounded four propositions about the way polls are reported in Britain:

1   However static public opinion actually is, the polls provide the media with a basis for giving the impression of flux, change and excitement. The more polls there are ... the more true this is.
2   However improbable a poll finding is, the media will publish a broadcast of it ... the more improbable a poll's finding is, the more likely the media will give it prominence.
3   However clear the election outcome and the election trend, polls allow the media to hedge their bets.
4   The duller an election is, the greater use of and prominence given to the polls.

There is truth if not poetry in these propositions, and there is a sound − if short-term − rationale for them. Sampling fluctuations will inevitably suggest change at first; it was not until half a dozen results were in in May 1979 that a static pattern became apparent, especially when the early RSL finding defied all attempts to fit it to a pattern. Improbable results make news; they may foretell a trend or shift in public opinion; they may suggest reaction to a promise, a broadcast or speech, a policy; they may even be right. The seventh poll saying nothing is changing is not news; the eighth suggesting change certainly is. Polls enable analytical assessments to be made. How will women, young people or one-eyed jacks vote? Will issues, leader or party determine their vote? Will the marginals topple/prop up the government? Polls provide grist for the journalist's mill; how fine he grinds it is part of the problem.

Pollsters in Britain take considerable pains to see that their clients get it right, do not overclaim on marginal shifts, insist on fieldwork dates, sample sizes etc., but in the end they have little control over headlines, story placement, length of coverage and less, much less, control over secondary coverage in other papers or on radio and television. Newspapers in Britain have conducted their own straw polls and run them without benefit of any statistical pretension, have bought bogus or biased polls and run them without disclaimer (rarely, I am happy to say) while one television programme once headlined, four weeks before election day, 'Tories to win with overall majority of 60+'.

Other problems that beset pollsters in dealing with the press include sub-editing after stories have been agreed with the reporter by sub-editors who do not understand (or care about?) the accuracy of the copy; well-meaning academics or other third parties who 'interpret', sometimes unknowledgeably, opinion poll results; inevitably short lead times and tight deadlines; space pressures; competitive 'scoops', 'poll of polls' averaging polls taken over the past week or so to suggest greater statistical reliability (theoretically so, but not if one poll is inaccurate as was the case in 1979); and perhaps my favourite, publication of amateur polls, such as that published by the *Daily Express* on 9 April 1979, which they described as 'An Express poll', taken among 500 coloured immigrants by amateur pollsters among an undefined sample during an undefined period, reporting to the first decimal place the answers to such questions as: 'Will you live in Britain forever?'.

Television has by its nature even more difficulty in reporting poll results, no matter how hard it tries. It is even shorter on copy deadlines and time to include the essential information of when the poll was conducted and other details. Perhaps the most creative use of polls in the May 1979 General Election was the Granada 500, described by Bob Self.[2] This series of programmes commissioned a survey of a bell-wether constituency in the heart of its coverage area to identify issues of concern to the electorate (which determined later programme content), establish an initial panel study data base, and recruit a representative sample of people to attend and take part in the programme series during the election campaign. Panellists were re-interviewed on several occasions, including on the weekend following the election.

One of the worst examples of television presentation' of polls was on BBC's *Nationwide* when commentators were asked to discuss poll findings illustrated by a large graphic display showing three polls' figures, two reallocating 'don't knows', one not. The interviewer neither understood nor was willing to listen to the arithmetic explanation of why the comparison was nonsense.

That polls make television news is shown by McKee,[3] who reported that ITN ran a poll story in their late news on two nights out of three during the 1979 campaign compared to just under 60% of main news bulletins in 1974. ITN also used poll data to determine programme focus on issues. Further, they asked the public how they thought television should cover the campaign and how election news — including polling results — could be improved. The first way they tried to improve poll data presentation was to put it into as clear a framework as possible, relating it to the campaign, clearly sourcing it both as to polling organization and to sponsoring newspaper, and blending in other information beyond voting intention, such as issues, leadership ratings, regional polls etc. The second initiative they took was to wrap up the week's polling coverage on Sunday night to point out trends and implications. They also ran an extended feature on how a polling organization works (as had the BBC earlier).

Some see the solution to the poll-press conflict at the sponsor level in having the copy written by the polling organization and commented on by journalists or even academics. This is better than the editorial licence taken by some papers when political reporters get lumbered with poll stories they are neither interested in nor understand, but leads in my view to dull and unrelated journalism. My own preference is for interested and knowledgeable journalists to develop a poll speciality and yet be able to bring in reaction, comment, analysis of impact and the like beyond what is possible or proper for a pollster to do.

Polls are the captive of the professionalism of the editor who commissions them, the journalist who writes them up, the graphics artist who designs the graphs to illustrate them, the sub-editor who subs the journalist's copy and writes the headline over it, and the pollster himself who must argue with any or all of the above to ensure that the pressures of the newsroom or the carelessness of the weakest link in the chain doesn't let him down.

Headlines

The 'bottom line' is most often the headline, and the headline is most often the weakest part of an opinion poll story. So often the editor has fought for the space and found the budget, the pollster has agonized over the questions and sent scores of interviewers to a carefully selected sample of hundreds or even thousands of people who have taken the time and trouble to give of their opinions, the computer has been programmed and has faithfully produced the figures, the journalist has strained and produced the copy, checked by the pollster, only to have a sub-editor put words into an eye-cathing headline that fits the space rather than the story. And we all know that many more readers will see the headline than will read the story, analyse the numbers or ponder on the graphics (if any).

Classic headline blunders include the following:

- implying change where no trend has been measured ('Blacks turn against violence');
- emphasizing the unimportant ('23% Don't Know');
- highlighting the insignificant ('SDP/Libs ahead of Labour' screamed a *Sunday Mirror* headline over the report of an insignificant 0.5% difference between the parties);
- quoting out of context ('Polls Useless says MORI Chief' in the *Manchester Evening News*, over a lead which began 'Most public opinion polls are useless in forecasting election results except when taken on the day of actual voting, an opinion poll chief claimed today.').

Text

Text is tricky when it comes to reporting polls. The average journalist is a wordsmith, not a number cruncher, yet he or she is asked to wrap words around statistical tolerances, percentage change over time, compare subgroups, possibly calculate swings and meet the deadline for copy in just two hours flat. It is a superhuman task; no wonder it so often goes wrong. The following are some of the most commonly encountered problems.

(1) Generalizing beyond the sample. It is too easy to extrapolate a survey finding from a region, or a sector of the public to the nation.

(2) 'Forgetting' the limitation of the poll. Journalists can too often 'forget to mention' that a survey was, say, done in April and that it is now September, or that it was a telephone poll in a country where only 75% of people are on the phone, or that there was a qualifying phrase to the question that was asked, or that it was released by a pressure group, or that it was done by Young Liberals, or that the question was 'filtered', that is, only asked of a subsample, etc.

(3) Spurious accuracy. Carrying the responses to one decimal point can suggest a degree of accuracy beyond the reliability of the data.

(4) Hyping the figures. The figures can be 'hyped' by repercentaging, leaving out the 'don't knows'. This is extremely bad practice except in election/referenda comparisons.

(5) Predicting the future: Poll results are a snapshot at a point in time and that time is when the fieldwork was taken, not three days, three weeks or three months into the future.

Foreign correspondents should not write that 'Latest polls in France forecast such and such an outcome'; they do not, they report the state of the parties on the day or days the interviews were taken, not the outcome a month hence. Worse are the subs who headline an impeccably written file reporting poll findings with a 'Polls Predict a Conservative Coalition Victory', as one newspaper did in January, when the French elections did not take place until 16 March. Full marks though for an excellent story sent to the *Observer* by Nigel Hawkes, their correspondent in Denmark, whose article on the upcoming Danish referendum reported that 'Opinion polls in Denmark show 50−55 per cent intending to vote "yes", 30−35 per cent "no" with the rest undecided. The most likely outcome, allowing for abstentions, is a majority of about 10 per cent in favour of the reforms. But indications are that turnout is not likely to be high, which could narrow the margin.' A sophisticated, yet simple, paragraph which captures the essence of what the prereferendum polls were showing.

(6) Concluding out of context. Sometimes questions are

asked which can be answered with a number of alternatives, such as:

In a 1970 survey of 500 students on 18 campuses in the Midwest, which was carried by several Midwestern newspapers, the researchers concluded that the new morality among collegians, at last in the Midwest, seems to have included at least a few 'old-fashioned' ideas in its code of ethics.

And, indeed, when asked about whether it is wrong for a married person to engage in sex with someone other than his or her spouse, or whether it is wrong for a woman to engage in sex with a man she knows casually, a majority of respondents said that it was 'almost always wrong' or 'always wrong'.

But when asked if it is wrong for a man or woman to engage in sex with someone he or she dates steadily or is engaged to, a majority of students said it was 'only wrong sometimes' or 'not at all wrong'.[4]

One newspaper chose to use the survey results as presented by the pollsters, and accepted in the headline the overall conclusion that college students' attitudes toward sex were rather conservative, even though that conclusion was based on about one-half the questions asked.

(7)   Telling half the story. It is a great failing of journalists (and politicians!) that they are prone to finding the figures that support the best/most interesting story most likely to startle the reader, whilst ignoring the follow-up responses which modify or contradict the 'sexy bits'.

(8)   Giving the answers but not the questions. Pollsters and some journalists work very hard to ensure questions are not simplistic, are complete, balanced and capable of being answered by typical respondents. Balanced questions include asking, for example, 'Do you favour or oppose . . .'. Some journalists and sub-editors delight in saving the two words 'or oppose', thus misleading the reader and inviting the letter writer protesting about the 'biased questions' in the poll. Worse is not reporting the question wording at all.

(9)   Not checking the facts. One of Britain's leading political commentators, Alan Watkins in the *Observer*, wrote several years after the 1983 General Election about the unreliability of

the polls, stating 'they underestimated the Alliance support at the last General Election'. I wrote to him to protest in the hope that he would set the record straight, saying,

> The Alliance got 26% of the vote, MORI, Marplan, NOP, Harris and Gallup all forecast an Alliance share of 26%. Only Audience Selection (by telephone) got the Alliance share wrong — and they overestimated Alliance support, not underestimated it.

Although I had a short but courteous reply which said 'Thank you for your letter. Wrong again', the pundit did not take the opportunity to run a correction in a subsequent column. It is no wonder there is a substantial proportion of the public who believe the polls always get it wrong when journalists who get us wrong — although when cheerfully admitting it privately — fail to correct the public record.

Tables

The presentation of tabular material gives rise to another set of problems.

(1)   Leaving out the questions. The tables are the best place to put the exact question wording of the question asked and answers offered. Too often the sub-editor sees this as an optional extra. It is not.

(2)   Numbers or percentages? Often it is confusing to the reader as to what is represented. If, as usual, 'all figures are percentages', why not say so as a footnote? It should be made clear whether the percentages read down or across to add to 100%. If the figures do not total to 100%, the table should say why (e.g. multiple answers accepted).

(3)   Source? Sometimes the tables are extracted or reprinted apart from the text; it is good practice to source the tables so that the reader can judge the reliability of the data and objectivity of the questions according to the reputation of the organization responsible for the survey. Also an indication should be given of to whom the interested reader can apply for further details of the methodology or the findings.

(4) Indicating the bases. When subgroups are reported, some caution needs to be taken of small sample bases; it is good practice, as indicated above, to indicate in the table the size of subsamples.

(5) Calculating trends. It is useful to the reader to be spared the effort of calculations. If a table includes a trend analysis, a column should be added that shows the change over time, for example,

Q. . . . . ?

	April 1986 %	Sept 1986 %	Change %
Approve	53	47	−6
Disapprove	44	43	−1
Don't know	3	10	+7
Difference	+9	+4	+5
Swing			−2½

Base: Adults in ABC   Source: XYZ

(6) Left to right. Most people read from left to right. It is amazing how editors and even pollsters think tables should read from right to left.

Graphics

By now an editor must be thinking that the difficulties of reporting polls outweigh their usefulness! And the next area — using graphics to represent poll findings — can cause even more grief.

The elements of the graphic are similar to those comprising a table: headline, question wording, data, base and source. There are three basic graphic techniques:

- Pie charts — showing share, when only one answer per respondent is permitted (i.e. when all the answers add to 100% and no trends are to be shown). *Tip*: Start at 12 o'clock and move clockwise, leave the 'don't knows' until last, and be careful to get the proportions right.
- Bar charts — showing distribution, especially when multiple responses are allowed and responses add to more than 100%. They can be used to show single trends, but this gets messy. *Tip*: Start with the largest response category and work downward. Be careful of leaving answer categories out and if you do so, say you have. Put the 'don't knows' at the bottom.
- Trend lines — best for showing trends over time. *Tip*: Remember, do not use equal spacing when the polls have been done at differently timed intervals. Also, be fair; do not squeeze the distance to overemphasize small changes.

One guaranteed way to get poor graphics is to keep the pollster and the graphic artist at arm's length and not let them discuss their work together. Another is to spring the poll findings on the artist an hour or so before deadline. It is best to involve the graphic artist early, even while the question working is being discussed.

Editorializing

Most polls have an editorial message for the enterprising leader writer. After all, it is vox populi that the poll represents, and the readers are interested in what their paper thinks about what they think. The pollster can be asked to identify the sponsoring paper's readers as a subgroup in the analysis — to see where they think the same as the public generally and where they differ. Leader writes should also lack at the poll's details; it is not only the main lead that lends itself to editorializing. And a final plea: do avoid the cliches — 'if this poll is to be believed ...', 'polls apart' and 'up the poll'.

Secondary reporting

When one paper picks up somebody else's poll, it still has an obligation to its readers to play it straight, and besides, the poll is almost certain to be copyright. Journalists should avoid reporting voodoo polls as if they were gospel truth, misrepresenting findings by glossing over suspect question wording, thin or skewed samples, or 'forgetting' to source them.

Using your pollster

When a newspaper or television programme embarks on publishing a series of commissioned opinion polls it is making a commitment to inform, educate and possibly even entertain its readers or viewers. The best models of media use of polls are those where a genuine collaboration of effort has been made between the pollster and the client. It takes time for the pollster to learn the paper's ways and for the paper's journalists and editors to learn the techniques and use of polls.

The typical pollster, if there is one, is likely to have an inquiring mind, a dedication to truth, a willingness to work day and night, week days and weekends, to meet deadlines, is well trained in his or her trade, knows the problems of the art of questionnaire construction and the techniques of sampling, will (or should) know where to cry 'halt' when cost pressures squeeze the sample size below a reliable level or shout 'whoa' when an over-eager journalist suggests a biased question wording.

What the pollster does not necessarily know about are house styles, journalistic methods, deadlines, layout problems, budget constraints and, especially, what is in the client's mind's eye as the story that will come out of the poll.

So, and I address these remarks directly to those who commission polls, discuss your ideas with your pollster. Talk about your paper's future plans. You can trust him; he is out of business very quickly if he can not keep a secret, and his obligations to his professional bodies, national, ESOMAR and WAPOR, require him to maintain his clients' confidences.

Consider teaching him about your business. Take him through the editorial process as if he were a new addition to the staff.

Consider paying your pollster a retainer over and above his fee for each poll; that way you will pay him for his time thinking how he can do a better job for you, coming up with ideas for polls, maybe even ideas for stories/features having nothing to do with polls; nor will he resent late night calls from your journalists checking on other people's polls and he will generally work on your behalf.

Establish a relationship of two, three, four or more years' duration. A contract and mutual commitment will give you both time to settle in and get to know each other. Appoint a journalist as the day-to-day liaison and give him or her time to visit the research institute to get to know the people there, perhaps go out with an interviewer for a few days, sit in on group discussions, see how the polling process works.

From time to time invite your pollster to sit in on your editorial conferences; make time for lunch or breakfast, say twice a year, to talk generally; give him your internal staff telephone list, exchange home phone numbers so you (and he) can be reached in off-hours; encourage his contributions.

Above all, check everything with him: clear copy, check tables and graphics, read over editorials and use him as your adviser. He will not usurp your editorial judgement or freedom, unless he's stupid, and if he is you will not keep him long. And do not expect him to do more than his trade will allow. Sometimes he is bound to get it wrong; worse, he may even miss a deadline, or ask a silly question, or misinterpret a finding. He is going to make a mistake sometime; he is only human. Forgive him occasionally, but if it happens often, get somebody else – and do not be afraid to try someone unknown; we all have to start somewhere.

Notes

1 Ivor Crewe, 'Improving, but Could Do Better', in Robert M. Worcester and Martin Harrop, *Political Communications: The General Election Campaign of 1979* (Macmillan, 1982).

2 Bob Self, 'The Granada 500: a Continuing Experiment in TV General Election Coverage', in Worcester and Harrop, *Political Communications*.

3 Paul Mckee, 'ITN's Use of Opinion Polls', in Worcester and Harrop, *Political Communications*.

4 G. Clevaland Wilhoit and David H. Weaver, *Newsroom Crude to Polls and Surveys* (American Newspaper Publishers Association, 1980).

15 Other Considerations

Same day polls

The development of 'same-day polls' as they are described in Britain or 'exit' polls, as they are referred to in America, has led to considerable criticism on both sides of the Atlantic. Some have been outrageously wrong: in the October 1974 General Election, BBC analysts were handed a forecast of a 150-seat Labour victory by the Louis Harris Organization who conducted polling station interviews in 85 English and 50 Scottish constituencies in an election that turned out to be a Labour win by a three-seat margin.

The difficulties in getting it right on the night are compounded for the polling organization by differential turnout, the reluctance of coloured voters to tell white interviewers how they voted, a comparative differential reluctance on the part of Conservatives to tell anyone how they have cast their ballots, the effect of snow or rain, the sampling of polling stations, the fact that polls are open in Britain from 7.00 am to 10.00 pm, and the effect of postal votes. Nevertheless, McKee[1] believes ITN have the system about right, and evidence is that their same-day polls are as accurate as many eve-of-poll surveys conducted in the more traditional way, although their 1987 performance of a forecast of a Conservative victory of 56 seats — while vastly better than the BBC's, based on Gallup, of 26 — was a long way from the actual result of 101.

It is argued that the result forecast ('the horse race') is of little value in the hour between the time the polls close and first declarations (usually received shortly after 11.00 pm). Newsmen say that the nation is waiting; that the pundits are discussing the day, the turnout, the weather, and this becomes an ingredient in the news mix. Opponents say that the record is spotty and adds little to knowledge or understanding. The alternative argument of the proponents is that in addition to the forecast of the outcome, same-day polls enable election analysts to determine the relevance of issues on voting behaviour, and other electoral factors which help to explain the outcome. How much this improves the same information from polls conducted the day before is hard to see given the relative accuracy of the two methodologies.

Worst polls

The worst kind of polls, and too frequently reported in and sometimes even conducted by the media, are self-selecting polls such as the coupon-poll in the *Daily Express* referred to earlier. The most famous is a poll carried out in 1936 by the *Literary Digest* in America. George Gallup tells the story:

In the decade preceding the 1936 presidential election, the Literary Digest conducted straw polls during elections and with a fair measure of success. The Literary Digest's polling procedure consisted of mailing out millions of post card ballots to persons whose names were found in telephone directories or on lists of automobile owners.

The system worked so long as voters in average and above average income groups were as likely to vote Democratic as Republican; and conversely, those in the lower income brackets – the have-nots – were as likely to vote for either party candidate for the presidency.

With the advent of the New Deal, however, the American electorate became sharply stratified, with many persons in the above average income groups who had been Democrats shifting to the Republican banner, and those below average to the Democratic.

Obviously, a polling system that reached telephone subscribers and automobile owners — the prerequisites of the better-off in this era — was certain to overestimate Republican strength in the 1936 election. And that is precisely what did happen. The Literary Digest's final pre-election poll showed Landon winning by 57% and Franklin D. Roosevelt losing with 43% of the two-party popular vote.

Landon did not win, as everyone knows. In fact, Roosevelt won by a whopping majority — 62.5% to Landon's 37.5%. The error, more than 19 percentage points, was one of the greatest in polling history.

The outcome of the election spelled disaster for the Literary Digest's method of polling, and a boon to the new type of scientific sampling which was introduced for the first time in that presidential election by my organisation, Elmo Roper's and Archibald Crossley's.

The Literary Digest had mailed out 10,000,000 post card ballots — enough to reach approximately one family in every three at that point in history. A total of 2,376,523 persons took the trouble to mark their post card ballots and return them.

Experiments with new sampling techniques had been undertaken by the writer as early as 1933. By 1935 the evidence was clear-cut that an important change had come about in the party orientation of voters — that the process of polarization had shifted higher income voters to the right, lower income voters to the left.

When the presidential campaign opened in 1936, it was apparent that the Literary Digest's polling method would produce an inaccurate figure. Tests indicated that a large majority of individuals who were telephone subscribers preferred Landon to FDR, while only 18 per cent of those persons on relief rolls favoured Landon.

To warn the public of the likely failure of the Literary Digest, the writer prepared a special newspaper article which was widely printed on July 12, 1936 — at the beginning of the campaign. The article stated that the Literary Digest would be wrong in its predictions and that it would probably show Landon winning with 56 per cent of the popular vote to 44 per cent for Roosevelt. The reasons why the poll would go wrong were spelled out in detail.

Outraged, the Literary Digest editor wrote: 'Never before has anyone foretold what our poll was going to show even

before it started ... Our fine statistical friend [George Gallup]
should be advised that the Digest would carry on with those old
fashioned methods that have produced correct forecasts exactly
one hundred per cent of the time.'

When the election had taken place, our early assessment of
what the Literary Digest poll would find proved to be almost a
perfect prediction of the Digest's final results – actually within
one percentage point. While this may seem to have been a
foolhardy stunt, actually there was little risk. A sample of only
3,000 post card ballots had been mailed by my office to the
same lists of persons who received the Literary Digest ballot.
Because of the workings of the laws of probability, that 3,000
sample should have provided virtually the same result as the
Literary Digest's 2,376,523 which, in fact, it did.

Through its own polling, based upon modern sampling procedures, the Gallup Poll, in the 1936 election, reported that the
only sure states for Landon were Maine, Vermont, and New
Hampshire. The final results showed Roosevelt with 56 per
cent of the popular vote to 44 per cent for Landon. The error
was 6.8 percentage points, the largest ever made by the Gallup
Poll. But because it was on the 'right' side, the public gave us
full credit, actually more than we deserved.

The Literary Digest is not the only poll that has found itself
to be on the 'wrong' side. All polls, at one time or another, find
themselves in this awkward position, including the Gallup Poll
in the election of 1948. Ironically, the error in 1936 – a
deviation of 6.8 percentage points from the true figure – was
greater than the error in 1948 – 5.4 percentage points. But the
public's reaction was vastly different.

The failure of polls to have the winning candidate ahead in
final results is seldom due to the failure of the poll to include
enough persons in its sample. Other factors are likely to prove
to be far more important.[2]

Unrepresentative, or 'voodoo' polls moved me to write a
letter to the British Market Research Society's Newsletter in
April 1984. This was responded to by the chairman of the
MRS Professional Standards Committee. I reproduce both
letters below.

Madam – Voodoo polling is becoming more than a joke. LBC
is running so-called 'polls' asking listeners to telephone their
answer to the question 'Do you favour the abolition of the

GLC?' One lady, in a letter to the *Evening Standard*, admits 'voting' three times and it would have been possible to have voted as many times as the line was free. The *Sun* newspaper prints a ballot asking their readers how they would vote in the miners' strike. And now Viewtel, the main news service on British Telecom's Prestel, is running what they describe as a 'straightforward opinion poll' asking viewers whether or not they would vote for Tony Benn if they lived in Chesterfield, prefacing their question with the following: 'What chance does the darling of the Labour left, Anthony Wedgwood Benn, stand of winning the crucial Chesterfield by-election in March? Will the moderates of this middle-of-the-road Labour constituency be ready to send to Westminster the man who was so decisively beaten at Bristol South East ...? Will the miners of Derbyshire be happy to endorse the left after the crisis for their union the overtime ban in the pits is producing? How does Labour's leader, Neil Kinnock, feel about the man in the party most likely to replace him as leader if the Tories win the next election? ... would you place your cross against Mr Benn's name?' In the event there were 103 votes for Benn, 197 against and four spoiled votes. Given that about 35,000 Prestel subscribers are 'on-line' of whom only a few thousand are in homes, the remainder being in offices, this may well be interpreted as an endorsement for Benn, given the incredible bias in the preface. I hope the MRS will express its dismay to Viewtel in no uncertain terms. Viewtel is owned by BMP, the parent company of the *Birmingham Post and Mail* and operates out of the Post and Mail building in Birmingham — R. M. W.

Madam — Robert Worcester is right to be disturbed by the growth of what he calls voodoo polling. To an extent it has to be our own fault. We have encouraged the trivialization of market research to the point where opinion polls are used as crutches by journalists unwilling or unable to make their own analyses of current issues. It can hardly be surprising that people come to the conclusion that polling is easy, something they can undertake for themselves. Nevertheless, the Society has to discourage the trend, through PR and education. Both areas are receiving substantial funding from Council. In the case of the Viewtel poll, we have written to the company asking for a clear declaration that their poll was a joke intended only for the entertainment of those who chose to take part. We have also asked that the exercise should not be repeated. Formal action of this kind is limited in its effectiveness. It needs reinforcement from members, who can make direct protest when they come across polls or other quasi-research which they feel are potentially damaging to the interests of MRS members. This is especially important − and may be especially effective − when the offence comes from a client or supplier. Does your company subscribe to Viewtel or advertise on LBC or in the *Sun*; do you conduct research for any of them; do you yourself work for one of them? If so, please do what you can. − Martin Collins, Professional Standards Committee.

None the less, these bogus polls persist, thrive and multiply. They bring their sponsors, perpetrators and, sadly, the rest of us into disrepute.

Telephone polls are a special case and are more often now used in the United States than not. This is one argument used for their introduction into Europe. For many uses this methodology is sound; in some, especially in election polls, the telephone poll must still be viewed with care. In March 1984 in *British Public Opinion Newsletter*,[3] I gave some of the reasons:

In Britain only 75% of households have telephones, while in the United States the ratio is 95%. In fact, telephone incidence here is now about 80%, but only just over half in unskilled working class (DE) households. More importantly, in each class segment, those with telephones are sociologically and, I contend, psychologically different from those without. There are other important differences. In the USA, Ma Bell has, for over two decades, offered WATS (Wide Area Telephone Service) lines to companies polling, selling, and otherwise communicating by phone. These are leased, 24-hours-a-day lines. Harris, in New York, can start polling at, say, 8.00 am on the East Coast and continue through to 1.00 am (NY time) interviewing on the West Coast, where it is only 9.00 pm (local time). In America, security has become a constraint on personal interviewing in many areas. Closed circuit television, automatic self-locking doors to blocks of flats and 24-hour guards are all commonplace. But, most importantly, there is a psychological difference to talking on the telephone. I grew up in America, with a phone in my ear. My family paid a monthly rental; all local calls were free. Every teenager in the USA spends hours on the phone; many have their own line. In Britain, especially in older working class households, there is a belief that a telephone is a means of emergency communication, not social intercourse. In America children don't ask permission to use the phone in most households. And finally, personal interviews are disproportionately more expensive than telephone interviewing in America. It is for these reasons, as well as the incidence of telephone ownership, that telephone polling has not developed as quickly in Britain as in America.

But perhaps the worst imports from the United States to Europe are the wholly self-serving 'Issues Surveys' or 'Opinions Surveys' conducted by the political parties. The party sends out questionnaires coupled with fund raising appeals and membership solicitations, and the unsuspecting victims who respond (signing their name) with their honest views on, say, housing, will find themselves the targets of mail shots at the next election detailing the party's candidate's views (neatly coinciding with the respondents' own) on housing.

Pressure groups have been known to engage in this manipulative activity as well. At a seminar in 1990 John O'Brien[4] reported on some 'opinion research' submitted to the Windscale inquiry which showed that 96% preferred an alternative energy policy to nuclear power. It was described in the *Financial Times* as 'a random survey among 1,200 people at 16 places in the UK'. He made the point in his talk that it was not 'random' in the statistical sense, but haphazard, involving a questionnaire that people filled in themselves and 'to top it all, the "survey" accepted up to four names on each reply' and a third of the forms returned came from Ballymena in Northern Ireland and Little Hayward, a small village in Staffordshire.

Banning polls

In Great Britain Parliament rules supreme. There are no written constitutional safeguards to freedom of the press. If Parliament were to ban publication of *The Times* tomorrow, *The Times* would cease publication. It is only the unwritten constitution that has endured for centuries that keeps Britain's press free, and the excesses of a parliamentary dictatorship in check. Parliament has been described as a 'democratic dictatorship' in that once a government is elected with a sizeable majority it can, so long as it keeps its own backbenchers in line, pass any legislation it wishes.

Thus, when the Speaker's Conference recommended in 1967 that polls be banned in the immediate period before polling day it had to be taken very seriously indeed. When an MP (a former academic) introduced a Private Member's Bill in the mid-1970s, it had to be cause for considerable concern, despite the fact that parliamentary advice was that 'it was not going anywhere'. One senior Labour NEC member expressed to me his desire to ban opinion polls for the fortnight before the election, explaining: 'it is sometimes necessary to be anti-democratic in order to save democracy ... Of course we would still continue to do our private polls', he said.

In France, for seven days preceding an election, Spain, for five, Portugal for 90 (sic) days and now Belgium, for 30 days, there are national bans on the publication of public opinion polls. In each country polls continue to be taken and influence the pronouncements of politicians, the pundits and leader writers and political commentators, the financial market makers and money manipulators; the only people who are kept in the dark are the public – denied access by politicians and legislators from the only objective measure of what the public thinks.

In 1985 a Council of Europe Parliamentary Assembly Committee held hearings in several European cities to investigate proposals for the 'harmonization' of laws to regulate the publication of polls. After extensive investigation, a review of the practices of its member governments, considerable testimony taken from academics, journalists and editors, legislators and government officials, the Parliamentary Assembly concluded 'therefore, having heard all the evidence, the Committee are not of the opinion that strong controls are shown to be desirable or necessary and there is no need or value in attempting international harmonization'.[5]

The Belgian ban, enacted early in the 1980s, was tested in 1985 by the news magazine *Knack* whose editor, Frans Verleyen, commissioned a poll and, four days before the General Election, published it in deliberate violation of the law; the law was also tested by *De Morgen* and *De Standard*. *Knack* quoted Article 18 of the 1831 Belgian Constitution in his defence, which states: 'The printed press is free; censorship can never be introduced . . .' In a commissioned article by a distinguished Belgian jurist *Knack* went further, arguing that the law banning polls was not only in violation of the Constitution by also Article 10 of the European Convention on Human Rights.[6]

The banning of publication of polls has been widely condemned and yet some countries do ban their publication and in other countries there are periodic attempts by well-meaning or publicity seeking politicians to enact legislation restricting them. It is up to editors and journalists, public opinion researchers and interested members of the public to be alert to these misguided efforts, to join together to defeat these attempts to limit press freedom and to use their ability to follow good practice in the conduct and presentation of polls to remove from their opponents any ammunition that they may derive from examples of bad practice.

In a free society polls cannot effectively be banned: if they were, the political parties would do even more polling than they do now − and leak it even worse than they do now. Secondly, stockbrokers, jobbers and other City 'gents' would do private polls and leak them (or make them up as they do now). Thirdly, foreign media would commission private polls in Britain and publish them overseas, and of course the results would be transmitted and reported subsequently in this country.

I reported in an article at the time (1979) that

This is the fourth General Election that I've been here that on the Monday and Tuesday before polling day the City has been swept by rumours that one or another of the major polls is coming out the following morning showing a sharp swing to Labour. In this election it was MORI, with a 3% Labour lead, in the *Express*. When it did not appear, it was 'being suppressed' and would appear in the next day's *Express*. The poll never existed, as we and the *Daily Express* told approximately 140 callers. Gallup, I later learned, was also plagued with calls from brokers and jobbers, some of whom were furious because Gallup and MORI would not give them the figures from our (non-existent) polls.

According to the *Financial Times*, these rumours wiped hundreds of millions of pounds off share prices. One paper especially well-read in the City, the *Evening Standard*,[7] carried the City headline 'Should We Ban Opinion Polls?', stating 'banning the polls would certainly make life easier for the fund managers and brokers ... a moratorium on polls before polling day would avoid the kind of panic we saw yesterday ...'. In the concluding paragraphs, the *Standard*'s City Editor said that it wasn't 'practical' to ban polls and that the City would just have to live with them. In the meantime, though, it cannot have helped our popularity, especially among those described in the City View column in the election-eve's *Daily Express*: 'Men have faced death with more dignity than displayed yesterday by some of those who thought their wallets were being threatened.'

Should we be worried that in a poll conducted just after the 1987 General Election MORI found 24% of the British public in favour of banning political opinion polls during General Elections? Of course we should, and do our best to convince them of the error of judgement of what helps and what harms democracy, just as we should be worried about the 25% who are in favour of the banning of party election broadcasts, and just as we should be worried about the 24% who are in favor of banning *all coverage of the election on radio and television*, and in this liberal society in which we live we should be worried about the 14% who are in favour of banning *all coverage of the election in the newspapers*.

The influence of polls

Finally, do polls influence voting behaviour? I believe they do, and I believe this to be a good thing. For many years pollsters and psephologists both in Britain and the United States have showed that the public took notice of the polls and that their voting behaviour was affected thereby. NBC tested (in California in the 1964 Presidential election) the effect of knowledge of computer-based forecasts of early (East Coast) returns on voting behaviour. Comparisons of behaviour between matched groups who saw the forecast and those who did not showed only slight differences.

After the 1979 General Election Butler et al.[8] concluded that 'there is some circumstantial evidence that polls may affect voting behaviour . . .' but 'there is clearly no general or consistent effect of the polls on voting behaviour'. The best evidence is from the study conducted for the BBC in May 1979 by Gallup which showed measurable support for the 'underdog' theory.

When you finally decide(d) which way to vote, were you influenced at all by what the opinion polls were saying?

	Yes %
All	3.0
Con	2.0
Lab	5.0
Lib	4.5

Source: Gallup BBC/Essex Survey

This showed that 3% of the electorate admitted to being influenced by reports of polls (67% had heard poll results), and the losers (Labour and Liberals) were over twice as likely to record this influence as those who voted for the winning Conservative party. This would suggest that the polls could have affected the votes of some 700,000 electors in the May 1979 General Election out of the 31 million who cast ballots, more than voted by post.

But it is in the by-elections that the influence of polls is clearest. In 1962, in Orpington, Kent, where a by-election was taking place, an NOP poll was published shortly before polling day which found that a majority of the constituency's electorate said they would vote for the Liberal candidate, Eric Lubbock, if they thought that he had a chance of winning. The poll showed that he did, and he subsequently won the seat.

Another example, also involving an NOP poll, was in the Bermondsey by-election just before the 1983 General Election when the constituency Labour party selected as their candidate Peter Tatchell, an allegedly homosexual, draft—dodging Australian left-winger, to stand in a traditional working-class, Catholic, dockside constituency which had been represented for many years by Bob Mellish, a right-wing Labour traditionalist and former Chief Whip, who backed an independent Labour candidate, the former leader of the local authority. An NOP poll published about ten days before the by-election showed a one point lead for Simon Hughes, the Liberal, over the independent Labour candidate, thus signalling to the good burghers of Bermondsey whom to vote for if they wished to ensure the defeat of Mr Tatchell. Simon Hughes won by a mile, and has held the seat ever since.

It is said that polls influence voting behaviour; they do, as I have said. It is also true in my judgement that newspapers and television influence elections. I have even heard it alleged that politicians have been known to affect the outcome, but on the last point I remain agnostic, though not an atheist.

Notes

1 Paul McKee, 'ITN's Use of Opinion Polls', in Robert M. Worcester and Martin Harrop, *Political Communications: The General Election Campaign of 1979* (Macmillan, 1982).
2 George Gallup, The *Sophisticated Poll Watchers Guide* (Princeton University Press, 1976).
3 Robert M. Worcester, 'Letter to Our Readers', British Public Opinion Newsletter, MORI, March 1984.
4 John O'Brien, *Opinion Polls — How to Judge Them*, Speech to MRS/Parliamentary Trust Seminar, January 1990.
5 Official Report, 37th Ordinary Session, Parliamentary Assembly, Council of Europe, 30 September 1985.
6 Dick Leonard, 'Belgian Leaders Should Read "Areopagitica"', *Wall Street Journal*, 18 October 1985.

7   Leith McGrandle, 'Should We Ban Opinion Polls?', *Evening Standard*, 2 May 1979.

8   David Butler, Howard Penniman and Austin Ranney, 'Opinion Polls and Elections', in *Democracy at the Polls* (American Enterprise Institute, Washington, DC, 198?).

Appendix
WAPOR Code of Professional Ethics and Practices

The purpose of the World Association for Public Opinion Research (WAPOR) is to establish a worldwide meeting ground for those working in the area of survey research. Through its activities, WAPOR unites the world of survey research within the universities and the world of survey research within private institutes — two worlds which far too often are still strictly separated. It is the express goal of WAPOR to bridge the gap existing between practitioners of social research in commercial institutes and theoreticians of the academe.

The first WAPOR council was composed of three university professors and three directors of private public opinion research institutes. In 1948 it was resolved to alternate the annual meetings between North America, Europe and Latin America. In the past years WAPOR has increasingly held its congresses together with other scientific associations such as the American Association for Public Opinion Research (AAPOR), the European Society for Opinion and Marketing Research (ESOMAR), the International Political Science Association (IPSA), the International Sociological Association (ISA), the International Communication Association (ICA), and the International Association for Mass Communication Research (IAMCR).

This custom of meeting with different international associations indicates that WAPOR and its members are, above all, interested in serving all disciplines of the social sciences by using the common method of survey research. WAPOR members practise their methods in the following fields:

- opinion and attitude surveys;
- audience research for papers, magazines, books, radio, television and broadcasting;
- market research;
- social research;

The limitation to public opinion research, as suggested by WAPOR's name, has thus practically become meaningless.

As early as 1948, Hadley Cantril pointed to the cleavage between the work of private institutes and universities in the field of survey research. Cantril saw the key to a full development of survey research methods in a mutually beneficial relationship of university institutes and survey research institutes. There is absolutely no reason to see this differently today. The distrust between the two worlds has even become greater, however, because it has become mutual.

The persistence of such tensions for over some thirty years is due to the peculiarities of survey research. Conducting surveys requires a relatively large staff of scientists, technicians and administrators as well as hundreds of interviewers. Such an apparatus has high overhead costs. On the other hand, only full financial independence can protect researchers from having to accept commissions under conditions which should be rejected from a scientific point of view.

For universities, the running expenses of the organization needed for surveys are too high. Thus social scientists in universities are in practice often unable to apply the methods of survey research in solving their problems. They often lack the data for analyses and they also often lack the confidence and experience to use this method which is much more complicated and requires more experience and information than many social scientists realise. On the other hand, this very data and experience has piled up in commercial survey research institutes outside of the universities. But the research practitioners in these institutes are generally under such pressure from their clients, financially and as regards deadlines, that barely any systematic development of methods or any analysis provoked by the scientific desire for knowledge could be achieved.

It was therefore one of WAPOR's foremost duties and desires to adopt a 'Code of Professional Ethics and Practices'.

Code of Professional Ethics and Practices of the World Association for Public Opinion Research

I *Introduction*

1 The World Association for Public Opinion Research (WAPOR), in fulfilling its main objective to advance the use of science in the fields of public opinion and marketing research and in recognition of its obligations to the public, hereby prescribes principles of ethical practice for the guidance of its members, and a framework of professional standards which should be acceptable to users of research and to the public at large.

2 In an increasingly complex world, social and economic planning is more and more dependent upon marketing information and public opinion reliably studied. The general public is the source of much of this information. Consequently, members of WAPOR acknowledge their obligation to protect the public from misrepresentation and exploitation in the name of research. At the same time, WAPOR affirms the interdependence of free expression of individual opinion and the researcher's freedom to interview.

3 Members of WAPOR recognize their obligations both to the profession they practise and to those who provide support for this practice to adhere to the basic standards of scientific investigation.

4 This code defines professional ethics and practices in the field of opinion and marketing research. Adherence to this code is deemed necessary to maintain confidence that

researchers in this field are bound by a set of sound and basic principles based on experience gained over many years of development.

II   *Rules of Practice between Researcher and Clients*

A   Responsibilities of Researchers

5   The objective study of facts and data, conducted as accurately as permitted by the available resources and techniques, is the guiding principle of all research.

6   In executing his work, the researcher shall make every reasonable effort to adhere exactly to the specifications proposed to and accepted by the client. Should the researcher find it necessary to deviate from these specifications, he shall obtain the client's prior approval.

7   The researcher shall in every report distinguish his actual data from observations or judgements which may be based on other evidence.

8   The researcher shall not select tools of data collection and analysis because of the likelihood that they will support a desired conclusion, if that conclusion is not scientifically warranted.

9   Whenever data from a single survey are provided for more than one client or when data are provided to several clients, the researcher shall inform each client of the fact.

10   In the course of a field survey, the researcher shall not reveal the name of his client to respondents or to anyone else, unless authorized by the client.

11   All information and material supplied by the client for the research must remain confidential.

12   Without prior consent of the client, no findings from the commissioned research shall be disclosed by the researcher. However, unless there is agreement to the contrary, the research techniques and methods, such as sampling designs, names of interviewers, field instructions etc., used for the study remain the researcher's property, if he has developed them.

13 Except by mutual consent, data shall not be sold or transferred by either the client or the researcher to parties not involved in the original contract work.

14 Unless it is customary or specifically agreed to the contrary, all punched cards, research documents (such as interviews and tests of sampled households) or any other material used in the field work shall be the property of the researcher. The practitioner is, however, required to provide for storage of this material for whatever period is customary in a particular country. This obligation shall be considered fulfilled by storage in a recognized data archive, if necessary, with restricted access.

15 Upon completion of a research study and after the researcher has submitted his final report, the client may request, according to previous mutually agreed specifications, a duplicate set of all punched cards prepared from the questionnaire, provided that the client shall bear the reasonable cost of preparation of such duplicates, and that respondents remain unidentified.

16 The practitioner shall be accurate in providing prospective clients with information about his experience, capacities and organization.

B Responsibilities of Clients

17 Potential clients asking for research proposals and quotations recognize that, in the absence of a fee being paid, such proposals and quotations remain the property of the researcher. In particular, prospective clients must not use the proposals of one practitioner competitively in order to obtain a lowering of the price from other practitioners.

18 Reports provided by the practitioner are normally for the use of the client and his agents. The researcher and the client shall agree in writing regarding the means of any wider dissemination of the complete or partial results of a research study.

In particular, it should be agreed that:

(a) The client shall ensure that any publication of survey results will not be quoted out of context or distort any facts or findings of the survey.

(b) The researcher must be consulted in regard to the form of publication and is entitled to refuse to grant permission for his name to be quoted in connection with the survey where he considers clause (a) has been violated.

C Rules of Practice Regarding Reports and Survey Results

19 Every complete report on a survey should contain an adequate explanation of the following relevant points:

(a) for whom the survey was conducted;

(b) the purpose of the study;

(c) the universe or population to which the results of the survey are projected;

(d) the method by which the sample was selected including both the type of sample (probability, quota, etc.) and the specific procedures by which it was selected;

(e) steps taken to ensure the sample design would actually be carried out in the field;

(f) the degree of success in actually carrying out the design including the rate of non-response and a comparison of the size and characteristics of the actual and anticipated samples;

(g) a full description of the estimating procedure used for all results which are reported including the sample size on which it was based and weighting procedures used to adjust raw data;

(h) a full description of the method employed in the field work;

(i) the time at which the field work, if any, was done, and the time span covered in collecting data;

(j) the findings obtained;

(k) (where the nature of the research demands it) the characteristics of those employed as interviewers and coders and the methods of their training and supervision;

(l) a copy of the interview schedule or questionnaire and instructions.

20 Technical terms shall be employed in a survey report in accordance with their commonly understood scientific usage.

III Rules of Practice between Researcher and Respondents

D Responsibility to informants

21 No informant or respondent must be adversely affected as a result of his answers or of the interviewing process. The practitioner shall use no methods or techniques by which the informant is put in the position that he cannot exercise his right to withdraw or refuse his answers at any stage of the interview.

22 No response in a survey shall be linked in any way to an identifiable respondent. The anonymity of respondents shall be respected, except in rare cases, with the respondent's specific permission. The interview method shall never be used as a disguise for a sales solicitation.

23 For field interviewers:

(a) Research assignments and materials received as well as information from respondents shall be held in confidence by the interviewer and revealed to no one except the research organization conducting the study.

(b) No information gained through a research activity shall be used, directly or indirectly, for the personal gain or advantage of the interviewer in his relations with the respondents.

(c) Field work shall be conducted in strict accordance with specifications. No field worker shall carry out more than one assignment in contact with the same respondents unless this is authorized by the research organization.

IV   *Rules of Practice between Researchers*

24   The principle of fair competition as generally understood and accepted should be applied by all researchers, even in cases where they may be the sole operators in their country.

25   In their personal and business relationships, researchers will be governed by the tradition of common respect among colleagues in the same profession.

26   No outside pressure, political or commercial, can be used by a researcher or research organization to justify violation of this code.

27   Members shall not try to turn to account or put into evidence the fact of their membership of WAPOR as a token of professional competence. Membership implies no guarantee of qualification, but it does imply acceptance of this code.

Excerpts from the Constitution of the World Association for Public Opinion Research

Article II – Purposes and Functions

Section 1: The purposes of the Association shall be:

(a)   to establish and promote contacts between persons in the field of survey research on opinions, attitudes, and behaviour of people in the various countries of the world, and

(b)   to further the use of objective, scientific survey research in national and international affairs.

Section 2: Functions and activities of the Association may include, but are not limited to, the sponsorship of meetings and publications, development of improved research techniques, encouragement of high professional standards, promotion of personnel training, coordination of international polls, and maintenance of close relations with other research agencies. Such agencies include the American Association for Public Opinion Research (AAPOR), the European Society for Opinion and Marketing Research (ESOMAR), and other regional professional research associations, as well as the United Nations Educational, Scientific and Cultural Organizations (UNESCO), other United Nations agencies, and private international organizations.

Article III Membership

Section1: Membership in the Association shall be as individual persons, not as representatives of organizations, nations, or other groups. There shall be two classes of members, full and associate.

WAPOR publishes both a newsletter and an academic journal, *The International Journal of Public Opinion Research* (Oxford University Press), and another of the benefits it can offer to its members is the subscription to *Public Opinion Quarterly* and *World Opinion Update* at reduced rates.

Bibliography

Abrams, M., *Social Surveys and Social Action* (Heinemann, 1951).

Berrington, H., 'Public Opinion Polls, British Politics, and the 1970 General Election', Political Studies Association Paper, Edinburgh, 1972.

Bradburn, N. and Sudman, S., *Improving Interview Method and Questionnaire Design* (Jossey-Bass, 1979).

Bogart, Leo, *Silent Politics: Polls and the Awareness of Public Opinion* (1972) reprinted as *Polls and the Awareness of Public Opinion* (Transaction Books, 1986).

Butler, D., *The British General Election of 1951* (Macmillan, 1952).

Butler, D., *The British General Election of 1955* (Macmillan, 1955).

Butler, D. and Kavanagh, D., *The British General Election of February 1974* (Macmillan, 1974).

Butler, D. and Kavanagh, D., *The British General Election of October 1974* (Macmillan, 1975).

Butler, D. and Kavanagh, D., *The British General Election of 1979* (Macmillan, 1980).

Butler, D. and Kavanagh, D., *The British General Election of 1983* (Macmillan, 1984).

Butler, D. and Kavanagh, D., *The British General Election of 1987* (Macmillan, 1988).

Butler, D. and King, A., *The British General Election of 1964* (Macmillan, 1965).

Butler, D. and King, A., *The British General Election of 1966* (Macmillan, 1966).

Butler, D., Penniman, H. and Ranney, A., 'Opinion Polls and Elections', in *Democracy at the Polls* (American Enterprise Institute, Washington, D.C., 1983).

Butler, D. and Pinto-Duschinsky, M., *The British General Election of 1970* (Macmillan, 1971).

Butler, D. and Rose, R., *The British General Election of 1959* (Macmillan, 1960).

Butler, D. and Stokes, D., *Political Change in Britain*, 2nd Edn. (Macmillan, 1969).

Cantril, H., *Gauging Public Opinion* (Princeton University Press, 1944).

Clemens, J., *Polls, Politics and Populism* (Gower, 1983).

Clemens, J., 'The Telephone Poll Bogyman: A Case Study in Election Paranoia', in I. Crew and M Harrop, (eds), *Political Communications: The General Election of 1983* (Cambridge University Press, 1986).

Crespi, I., *Public Opinion, Polls and Democracy* (Westview Press, 1990).

Disraeli, B., *Sybil* (Oxford University Press, 1981).

Durant, H., 'Behind the Gallup Poll', *News Chronicle*, 1951.

Gallup, G. (ed), *The Gallup International Public Opinion Polls, Great Britain, 1937–1975* (Random House, 1976).

Gallup, G., *The Sophisticated Poll Watcher's Guide* (Princeton University Press, 1976).

Hodder-Williams, R., *Public Opinion Polls and British Politics* (Routledge and Kegan Paul, 1970).

Kavanagh, D., 'Public Opinion Polls', in, D. Butler, H. Penniman and A. Ranney (eds), *Democracy at the Polls* (American Enterprise Institute, 1983).

Kish, L., *Survey Sampling* (John Wiley, 1965).

Kovach, B., 'A User's View of the Polls', *Public Opinion Quarterly*, 44, 1980.

Lazersfeld, P., 'Public Opinion and the Classical Tradition', *Public Opinion Quarterly*, 21, 1957, pp. 39–53.

Lippman, W., *Public Opinion* (Macmillan, 1922).

Lippman, W., *The Phantom Public* (Harcourt Brace, 1925).

McCallum, R. and Readman, A., *The British General Election of 1945* (Oxford University Press, 1947).

McCarthy, M., 'Thatcher's Children', series published in *The Times*, 1–4 September 1986.

Moser, Sir Claus, *Survey Methods in Social Investigation* (Heinemann, 1958).

Nicholas, H.G., *The British General Election of 1950* (Macmillan, 1951).

Noelle-Neumann, E., 'Public Opinion and the Classical Tradition: a Reevaluation', *Public Opinion Quarterly*, 43, 1979, pp. 143–56.

Payne, Starley, The Art of Asking Questions (Princeton University Press, 1951).

Penniman, H. (ed.), *Britain at the Polls: The Parliamentary Elections of 1974* (American Enterprise Institute, 1975).

Penniman, H. (ed.), *Britain at the Polls 1979* (American Enterprise Institute, 1979).

Penniman, H., *Britain at the Polls 1983* (American Enterprise Institute, 1985).

Pimlott, B., 'A Consensus that has its Roots in Tory Failure', *Guardian*, 19 August 1986.

Rose, Richard, 'Political Decision-making and the Polls', *Parliamentary Affairs*, XV, Spring 1962, pp. 118–202.

St John de Crevecoeur, J.M., *Letters from an American Farmer* (Signet, 1963).

Teer, F., and Spence, J., *Political Opinion Polls* (Hutchinson, 1973).

Webb, N., 'The Democracy of Opinion Polls', ESOMAR/WAPOR Seminar on Opinion Polls, Bonn/Bad Godesberg, FRG, 1979.

Wilhoit, G. and Weaver, D., *Newsroom Guide to Polls and Surveys* (ANPA, 1980).

Worcester, R., 'Pollsters, the Press, and Political Polling in Great Britain', *Public Opinion Quarterly*, 44, 1980.

Worcester, R., 'History of Political Polls in Great Britain', Paper presented to the Silver Jubilee Market Research Society Conference, 1982.

Worcester, R., 'Don't Disregard the Power of the Polls', *The Director*, June 1983.

Worcester, R., 'The British General Election 1983', Paper presented to the World Association for Public Opinion Research, Barcelona, Spain, 27 August 1983.

Worcester, R. (ed.), *Political Opinion Polling: An International Review* (Macmillan, 1983, St Martins Press, 1983).

Worcester, R., *British Public Opinion: The General Election of 1983* (MORI, 1983).

Worcester, R., 'Britain at the Polls 1945–1983', *Public Opinion Quarterly*, 48, Winter 1984, pp. 824–33.

Worcester, R., 'Letter to Our Readers: Trying to Overcome "Position Bias"', *British Public Opinion Newsletter*, March 1985.

Worcester, R., 'Letter to Our Readers: Re: Public Opinion Polls (Prohibition at Election Times)', *British Public Opinion Newsletter*, October 1985.

Worcester, R., 'Letter to Our Readers: Americans in Tripoli', *British Public Opinion Newsletter*, April 1986.

Worcester, R., 'Swings and Falls that Spawned a Landslide', *The Times*, 13 June 1987.

Worcester, R., 'Polls Apart', *New Socialist*, Summer 1988.

Worcester, R., 'Population Change: Changing Population and Changing Attitudes', paper presented to the Civil Service Top Management Programme, 7 July 1988.

Worcester, R. and Downham, J. (eds.), *Consumer Market Research Handbook*, 3rd edn (Elsevier North Holland, 1986).

Worcester, R. and Harrop, M. (eds), *Political Communications: The General Election Campaign of 1979* (*Macmillan*, 1982).

Index